Ukraine

Chronicle of the Events of the War in Ukraine

(The History and Legacy of Ukraine From the Middle Ages to Today)

Travis Sedlak

Published By **Phil Dawson**

Travis Sedlak

All Rights Reserved

Ukraine: Chronicle of the Events of the War in Ukraine (The History and Legacy of Ukraine From the Middle Ages to Today)

ISBN 978-0-9950957-8-6

No part of this guidebook shall be reproduced in any form without permission in writing from the publisher except in the case of brief quotations embodied in critical articles or reviews.

Legal & Disclaimer

The information contained in this book is not designed to replace or take the place of any form of medicine or professional medical advice. The information in this book has been provided for educational & entertainment purposes only.

The information contained in this book has been compiled from sources deemed reliable, and it is accurate to the best of the Author's knowledge; however, the Author cannot guarantee its accuracy and validity and cannot be held liable for any errors or omissions. Changes are periodically made to this book. You must consult your doctor or get professional medical advice before using any of the suggested remedies, techniques, or information in this book.

Upon using the information contained in this book, you agree to hold harmless the Author from and against any damages, costs, and expenses, including any legal fees potentially resulting from the application of any of the information provided by this guide. This disclaimer applies to any damages or injury caused by the use and application, whether directly or indirectly, of any advice or information presented, whether for breach of contract, tort, negligence, personal injury, criminal intent, or under any other cause of action.

You agree to accept all risks of using the information presented inside this book. You need to consult a professional medical practitioner in order to ensure you are both able and healthy enough to participate in this program.

Table Of Contents

Chapter 1: Kievan Rus 1

Chapter 2: Medieval Militaries In Eastern Europe 15

Chapter 3: The Wars Of Daniel And Leo I 27

Chapter 4: The Rise Of Lithuania 39

Chapter 5: The Knights Engaged In The War Against 56

Chapter 6: Sigismund Was A Victim Of Huge Losses 75

Chapter 7: Background And Context 94

Chapter 8: Events Leading To The Conflict 107

Chapter 9: Pro-Russian Separatism In Eastern Ukraine 133

Chapter 10: Accusations And Denials Of Russian Involvement 150

Chapter 11: International Response And Diplomatic Efforts 168

Chapter 1: Kievan Rus

According to the chronicles of the Rus, Tales of Bygone Years as well as The Primary Chronicles, the city of Kiev was established by Polyanians. Polyanians: "While the Polyanians resided separately and ran their families (for in the past, prior to the brothers, there already were Polyanians who each was a member of his own people living in his own land, in charge of his family) Three brothers: Kiy, Shchek, and Khoriv Their sister was christened Lybed.' Kiy resided on the hill that is where there is now the Borichev route is today located, while Shchek lived on the hill that is now known as Shchekovitsa and there was a third Khoriv and the hill was called Khorevitsa. They constructed a town, and called it Kiev in honor of their elder brother. In the city was an area of woods and a huge pine forest, where they would use to capture wild animals. They were smart and prudent. They were known as Polyanians as well as there are Polyanians descendents of them in Kiev today. day."[44

The state of the new era was Russia or, more commonly as in the West, Ruthenia - was one of the biggest in Europe. The ties that it established between the Baltic as well as the Black Sea made it wealthy and strong. It also established trade relations with Constantinople as the capital city of the powerful Roman (Byzantine) Empire. The city was referred to as Tsargorod (Caesar's city) and was able to access the riches that were found in the East. The Grand Prince Vladimir the Great introduced Byzantine Christianity to Russia in the latter part of the 10th century. He made Russia as a strict Christian state. In the following century The Rus had a wealth of influence, yet was not surrounded by neighbors who were dangerous. The west was dominated by the Catholic Hungarians and Poles. They were bordered by the Baltic by Finns, Latvians, Estonians, Latvians and other tribes. The south and to the east there was a range of Turkic nomadic tribes, one of the most popular being Pechenegs and the Cumans. They were a part of the Steppes which is today south Ukraine as well as the Crimean Peninsula. The Rus constantly fought against them, however neither of them, as well as their neighbor had the power to take down the Kievan State.

In 1037, the Grand Prince Yaroslav who was exalted in Ukrainian as well as Russian traditions for being a wise holy and a learned leader, secured Kiev against enemies as reported by The Primary Chronicle: "Yaroslav constructed the citadel of Kiev close to at the Golden Gate. The Metropolitan Church of St. Sophia and which is the Church of the Annunciation over the Golden Gate, and also the Monastery of St. George as well as the monastery that was founded by St. Irene. In his time in the era of his death, the Christian faith flourished and spread, and monks' numbers increased as new monasteries were brought to existence. Yaroslav was a fan of religious institutions and was extremely devoted to priests and especially monks. He devoted himself to reading books that he read continuously all day and at night. He brought together a number of scribes and also translated Greek to Slavic. He wrote and compiled numerous books in which the those who believed in God were educated and received religious instruction. As one man ploughs the soil, another seeds, while people reap and consume abundantly the prince. His father Vladimir ploughed and tilled the land after he was able to educate Rus' through baptism, and this prince also nourished the hearts of his followers by writing the word which we then reap the fruits of our labor by learning from books. Great is the gain from book-learning."[5[5

It was believed that the Rus state was run by several Dynastic families. Each was led by an individual prince (kynaz) who was ruled by his personal entourage. Principal landowners offered their military services in exchange for their land. In the Grand Prince's reign, (Velikiy Kynaz) of Kiev had supremacy over other princes due to its historical significance and also commanded the Russian army during the war.

It's an error to relate the culture that existed in medieval Rus to the one of post-modern Russia which was centred around Moscow. It wasn't like the autocratic Muscovite empire. The government was more democratic, and, in a range of instances, most notably the city-states of

Novgorod in the city of Novgorod, cities had power via the city council, or an veche. In contrast to Muscovy (and Western Europe at the period) the medieval Russian the peasants had no cost, and in principle, were equal with the prince. Capital punishment was uncommon and, at a certain point the law was completely eliminated.

Kievan Rus declined due to the demise of the Grand Prince Yaroslav I Vladimirovitch in 1054. The son, Iziaslav, was unpopular as the Grand Prince and was dependent on Poles to support the throne. He was the husband of Gertrude of Poland who was the sister to the Polish Duke Casimir I, and, following his exile from Kiev after 1069, returned to Kiev in 1069, as the commander of the Polish army. This is the point in the history of mankind that the issues of Poland as well as the territories that would later become Ukraine are entwined.

The tragic reigns (for the three times he was in power) of Iziaslav and the encroachment from Poland and the Cuman invasions threw Kievan Rus to turmoil. The Grand Prince was battled over between the different factions of the Rurik Dynasty. Between the death of Iziaslav in 1078 until 1237, the Mongol invading Russia during 1237. There were only 18 Grand Princes with the reigns lasted for 31 years, which is they had multiple reigns after having been exiled by rivals, and then reinstated. Through this period of chaos, the Grand Princes ceased to have any influence, and regional princes ran their respective principalities in the role of sovereigns who were independent.

At the time of the Mongol invasion, the land in what's now referred to as Ukraine were held with four majorities. Kiev was the ruler of the Ukrainians who lived that straddled the Dnieper (in today's Moldova) and Pereyaslav, who held the central Ukraine. Novgorod-Seversk ruled the northern region near the Dnieper. The Principality of Galicia Volhynia West of Kiev is the biggest and strongest of the south Rus states. For the time it was in contention to become the Great Prince of Rus. It was one of the more western among the Rus principalities with connections with the neighboring Poland as well as Hungary. In fact, both competed for control over the territories. The Steppes to the west of Dnieper was held by the Cumans as well as various other Turkic tribesmen. Later, when the Mongols came, they would join with the invaders and become The Golden Horde.

It's important to remember in this context that Ukraine isn't a new invention. It translates to "borderland," which is the reason English natives have for many years were referring to the country in the form of "The Ukraine." Ukrainians are against using the word "definite" as a derogatory to their sovereign rights. The earliest known usage of the word dates to 1187 and is related to prince Volodmyr of Pereyaslavl who's death was the cause for "Oukrainia" to groan. The name was used to refer to any frontiers of military importance regardless of the geography similar to the English "march" or German "mark," which became a part of this region by the 16th century.

The Ukrainians initially encountered Mongols in 1223, when their troops attacked along the Dnieper River. A group of Mstislav III of Kiev, Yuri II of Vladimir-Suzdal as well as Daniel of Galicia-Volhynia fought undetermined numbers of troops against 20.000 Mongols on the Kalka River on May 31. It was a devastating Russian loss, however the victors didn't pursue their attack. Instead, they moved to the north toward Volga and defeated the Bulgars that ruled the area. Returning to their region however, 1239 was the year after having first destroyed the northern Rus during the battle of Sit River. They destroyed their way towards Crimea before turning to the north, heading towards Pereyaslavl. The Mongols burned the city. In the nearby Chernigov was similarly affected as did Kiev. Kiev was taken over by an extended siege that began in 1240.

The papal representative to the Mongol court outlined the destruction: "They [the Mongol] took on Rus', where they destroyed a great deal of fortresses, cities and towns and killing people; they also took over Kiev which was the capital city of Rus'. After having occupied the city for a lengthy duration, they conquered its occupants and put them to the death. As we walked across the land, we saw a lot of skulls and the bones of deceased people lying in the dirt. Kiev was once a vast and affluent town and is now diminished to almost nothing in the sense that currently there are only two hundred homes that are there, and people living there are held in absolute slaves. From there and fighting wherever they traveled The Tartars have destroyed the entire region of Russia."[7[7.

Batu Khan, the Mongol ruler, Batu Khan, continued through Galicia and destroyed the territory of its prince Daniel on his way towards Hungary as well as Poland. The Mongols were not able to absorb and conquer their new territories. They instead settled on the Lower Volga and merged with the Cumans, as well as with others Turkic nomadic groups to create known as the Golden Horde. Its capital was Sarai the

Golden Horde allowed lost princes to hold their land, but only with the approval from the Great Khan. They were only able to rule upon receiving the yarlyk licence granted by the Great Khan in Sarai. They were obliged to pay the requisite tribute and failure to honor this obligation was met with the most brutal punishment. They were known as the Golden Horde. Golden Horde would burn defiant cities down to the ground and massacre their citizens.

The title Grand Prince of Rus was a present of the great Khan. He utilized it to be in control of his Russian princes. The title no longer had the power it was once possessed, however it could be a symbol of status and permitted the person who held it to take tributes on the khan's behalf and keep a large part to him. Disputs about succession led to the princes being divided, and consolidated the power that was the Golden Horde.

In 1241, all princes from the Rus surrendered to the Golden Horde. Novgorod in from the North was among of the towns that escaped destruction, however its residents remained silent and did not put up fighting. One exception was Daniel who was from Galicia. Following the invasion of the Mongols invaded his land, he was able to return a sense of authority. The Mongol leadership was more worried with going back in Karakorum in Mongolia after the demise of Ogedai Khan, successor to Genghis Khan. The Mongols' troops retreated from Poland as well as Hungary across Daniel's land. They pursued them until Daniel gained control of the capital city of the Rus, Kiev. Galicia and Volhynia have escaped in the meantime in the meantime. Daniel was aspired to being the

Grand Prince of all the Rus. However, he was in need of help and his eyes turned toward the West.

Chapter 2: Medieval Militaries In Eastern Europe

There were a variety of main powers in the period including the Rus and the Golden Horde, Lithuania, Poland, Hungary and the Teutonic Knights. Russian armies were comprised of higher class druzhina as well as the voyi of the commoner. The druzhina was an individual retinue belonging to the prince. the prince chose not just warriors as well as governors and administrators. It was an army that remained in place and therefore was able to be called upon with very little notice. The druzhina comprised boyars who, as knights from the west of Europe were granted lands and positions in exchange for duty in the military. The 14th century saw the roles of boyars grew, until they were able to hold authority independently from the druzhina. They would fight on horseback using helmets and chainmail, and used swords, maces, or lances. Light cavalry equipped with composite bows was used, although they were more likely to be Turkic soldiers.

The voyi were recruited from the population of the area. They might be urban militias drawn from local old people or the city council. The princes preferred to depend on levies from peasants equipped with simple spears and an axe. Although they had no training and did not have the money to arm themselves, they were able to have more loyalty than militias, who were likely to only fight in their local town.

The Mongol invasion had a significant impact on The Russian military. Fortifications with strong fortifications were important and so did the use of crossbows and plate armor. The first handguns were introduced during the 14th century however, they weren't commonly utilized.

The Tartar masters of the Rus were largely dependent on cavalry with light archers. They were extremely mobile and adept and their preferred tactic was to slug the opponent to exhaustion instead of launching an open strike. In the face of heavily armored boys and Western knights they continuously shot and retreated until their opponents had exhausted. Tartar bows could reach a distance around 250m more than the English longbow. The Lancers then fell on the enemy who was too weak to fight. Through these methods an army from the Golden Horde could defeat an opponent that was several times larger. Feigned attacks were the most popular tactic used as it was able to draw enemy units away from the formation. Their armors were typically made of felt, fur or leather that did not hinder speed. However, it could be complemented with chains and scale.

The Golden Horde habitually employed terror strategies. They rarely released prisoners. They systematically killed people in a captive town. They didn't torture people, and commanding officers were given specific numbers of citizens who were to be executed. The goal of this horrifying procedure was to scare the population into submission and to intimidate opponents. The practice was, in vastly, extremely successful.

When the Mongol invasion of Russia as well as the growth of Ruthenia, Lithuania was a relatively young country. In contrast to the Slavs who lived around the Lithuanians adhered to their traditional pagan faith as a result of which they were continuously attacked by Teutonic Knights. The Mongols were also raiding their territory, causing 20 cunigaiksciai (translated "dukes") to pick Mindaugas to be their grand Duke. While Mindaugas was the ruler who was baptized, the vast majority of his people as well as many of his successors the next 200 years were devoted to the shamanist tradition. This was what made Lithuania distinct as the sole organised state within Europe that wasn't Christian.

Lithuanian tribal warriors enjoyed a variety of advantages over Teutonic Knights and Ruthenians. They generally had light armor and had a good understanding of mobility. They were able to navigate the forest and marshy terrain more efficiently and relied heavily on ambush and stealth. Lance-wielding soldiers were able to move through the forest and surprise the enemy and disappear in the woods. They were different from their Tartar enemies and were more in their ability to defeat these enemies in comparison to their German as well as Russian neighbours. When the Lithuanian state grew into Volhynia and

Galicia during the 14th and 15th centuries, the military comprised the boyar cavalry, and incorporated more traits of its neighbours.

When the Mongol attack and the Mongol invasion, the military of Poland changed. Its foundation was the druzhina. This was the same as in Rus principalities. However in the 11th century, west feudalism came into play. Druzhina soldiers were substituted with knights who offered the military service to gain their land. Knights were required to keep their own armour and keep themselves ready for war and they were less expensive than monarchs as were the higher nobles who kept their own retinues.

The townsfolk and serfs comprised part of the infantry unit in the middle ages Polish military. They were also expected to supply their own gear as well as serf soldiers generally had lower standard compared to the urban militias. Infantry were armed with siege weapons, defended baggage trains, defended fortresses, and provided assistance to the cavalry heavy. Infantry mounted served as light reconnaissance troops and cavalry that was skirmish.

The high Duke (King in 1295) of Poland had the right to summon all the army of fighting to defend the kingdom. The levy was referred to as the Pospolite Ruszenie. If the soldier wanted to go on a mission outside Poland it was usually forced to pay the troops.

With their weapons, armors, and clothing Polish knights were modelled after their counterparts from Western Europe. They were equipped with lances, swords, and maces and also wore chains, and were later enhanced with plate. At the end of the 14th century the helmets of Norman style came to be replaced with the huge helm, which completely covered the head. Polish shields and surcoats were decorated with symbols and colors of the heraldry similar to medieval knights of the west.

As with similar to the Polish like the Polish, as with the Polish, Hungarian military was also feudalized but a lot of the original Magyar archers and horses remained. They were similar to those of the Mongol cavalry, however they were shattered by who invaded during the battle of Mohi in 1241. The Mongols were not able to remain within Hungary however, the king's power was greatly less. Barons took on the responsibility to defend themselves and their power increased. They had their knightly retinues that are similar to Druzhinas from their respective Russian and Polish nobles. The 14th century was when the monarchs of Hungary had succeeded in harnessing the power of barons and also augmented their army by deploying Cuman as well as South Slavic mercenaries.

The last of the military units to be taken into consideration is that of the Teutonic Knights, or to make use of the full name for the organization, Brothers who are members of the German House of Saint Mary in Jerusalem. Similar to other military orders that were founded in order to safeguard Christian pilgrims from Jerusalem in the Holy Land, but moved to Europe in the aftermath of the Saracens captured Jerusalem. They transferred the order to Transylvania and they tried to seize away from Andrew II of Hungary, which was exiled in 1225. The knights later established the state of Prussia by capturing violently the land of indigenous pagans who they massacred and then enslaved. It was believed that the members of the group were bound by vows of chastity, poverty and obedience. They were expected to adhere to the principles of the crusader as well as knight, i.e. protection of the less fortunate and infirm. But in reality, they were derived from unemployed members of the German Aristocracy, who were seeking riches and property as well as not much to differentiate them from the barons who racked up a hefty dowry in their countries of origin.

The top of the Order below the pope was known as the Grand Master. And the principal unit of administrative control was the Commandery. Every commander acted like the feudal baron by demanding taxes and other services, and executing justice. Teutonic warriors took their cues from knights from the west with regard to armor, armaments and strategies. They stood out with a dark black cross on white sari. The knights of the professed were an insignificant portion in their Teutonic army, the vast majority of them were gray-coated Sariant of brothers serving in the army, who didn't take vows of solemnity, nor did the aristocratic locals who were from Germany.

The 13th century was when in the 13th century, Teutonic Knights subdued Prussia and Livonia and gained a repute that was frequently noted by the other members of their religious. A Franciscan friar wrotethat "The members who belong to the Teutonic order can be very troublesome to the conversion of unbelievers because of the battles they constantly start as well as the fact that they want to rule them completely. ... Pagans have at many times been able to accept the peace faith after the sermon, however those belonging to the Teutonic order are not willing to let this happen, as they want to subjugate them, and convert them to slavery."[88.

The fervor of the Teutonic Knights brought them into perpetual conflict with Lithuanians and remain their only neighbors of pagan origin (the descendants of Mindaugas went back to pagan religion). Since knights were not able to get married, they required an ongoing flow of knights to support the Order. However, knights were only welcome when there were people who were heathen, to rob and change their religion. So, the retaking of Lithuania proved crucial to ensure the continued existence of the Order. Yet, Lithuanians could not be stopped to resist. In fact, the their pagan Lithuania was transformed into a powerful state during the fifteenth century. This had significant implications for Galicia as well as for the area of Kiev.

Chapter 3: The Wars Of Daniel And Leo I

The first attempts of Prince Daniel to reach out to the West received a hostile response. An Hungarian-Polish force took advantage of the Mongol destruction and encroached on Galicia at the time of 1245. The army was headed by Rostyslav who was the prince exiled of Halych. Bela IV of Hungary was his father-inlaw as well as brother-inlaw of Boleslaus V of Poland and Boleslaus V of Poland, who wanted to make sure that their big neighbor from becoming weak. Rostyslav was beaten by Daniel in the Battle of Yaroslav located 130 km to the to the west of Lvov. Daniel's victory confirmed his position and raised his status in the eyes of his neighbors to the west. To increase his stature the king traveled to Sarai and pledged his allegiance in the direction of Batu Khan, who was amazed by his performance. "You are one of ours now," the Khan informed him following the offer of an oath drink that was Goat's milk fermented. 9 Daniel was able to praise his tyrannical masters knowing that the Golden Horde was too far from Galicia Volhynia in order to not influence its activities. Daniel used the time of peace to expand his state, by constructing fortresses, cities and towns and welcoming artisans and merchants to join him from Germany, Poland and Armenia. The laws he enacted were to establish Jews and to protect them, and to protect the peasants from the aristocratic oppression. He also resisted the aristocratic influence through the creation of a corp of peasant soldiers.

Daniel was aspired to become the Grand Prince of the entire Russia and to free himself from the Tatar yoke, and to create Galicia the central political region of Russia. His goals were in perfect harmony with the pope Innocent IV. The Pope had for a long time kept ties with the Mongols as well, and his goal was to bring them to Christ. Mongols into Christianity. If he failed, he'd launch a campaign against the Mongols. In 1245 He sent envoys over in the direction of Batu Khan, 'the Emperor of the Tartars asking that cease the killing of Christians and also convert. Not surprisingly, Batu replied by demanding acceptance to Innocent as well as the other kings of Christendom. Innocent wrote letters to Russian princes, urging the princes to leave Byzantine Christianity and accept the Catholic Church. In 1245, the Grand Prince Yaroslav II who ruled in Vladimir located in northwestern Russia thought about it, but he was poisoned by Toregene the regent of Khan Guyuk, her son Khan Guyuk, during a trip to Sarai in 1245.

Prince Daniel began to join the fight and, in an effort to secure the backing of the Catholic West Prince Daniel was willing to recognize Innocent as the head of the Galician Church. As a result In doing so, he broke with the other princes, who recognized Innocent as the Byzantine patriarchal rector of Constantinople as their supreme leader. Around 1253 Innocent dispatched his personal legate Opizzo Fieschi make him the to be the King of Ruthenia (Rus) in his capital city, Dorochochyn (now located in Poland). Daniel was said to complain that he was expecting an army from the west[10However, he was a bit underestimating the west's interest in fighting to defeat the Mongols. He waged war in the battle against Golden Horde alone, but still had limited successes. In 1256, he rid both the Horyn as well as Sluch valleys of troops and built fortifications. The reason he was successful is because he adopted Mongol strategies, weapons and even military clothing. Following his death there was a

Tatar attack to seize towns like Volodymyr as well as Lutsk was stopped. He was about to lead an army to the eastern part of Ukraine in the spring of 1898 when an force from Sarai was spotted with the aim to destroy Ruthenia. He was ordered to bow to the threat of total destruction of his homeland. Knowing that he was unable to fight the battle without support from westerners, Daniel reluctantly complied. Daniel was ordered to tear down his fortifications and then to kneel before the khan of Sarai.

Daniel's humiliation rescued Ruthenia and ensured it the strength and stability it has enjoyed for years to come. The king continued his reign for the duration of his time expanding his territory and consolidating his ties with the West with an apparent desire to challenge his Golden Horde again. He got married with the son of his Svam to the girl who was the daughter from Mindagaus I, who was the first Grand Duke in the advancing Lithuanian state. Lithuania. Similar to Daniel the Mindagaus family, Mindagaus became a convert his faith to Catholicism (from paganism) and was awarded a crown from the hands of the papal legate. The reason he did so was similar to the motives. While Daniel was under threat from his own Golden Horde, Mindagaus was in danger by the military order of Teutonic knights who were based in Prussia. Daniel tried to get married the son of his Roman in marriage to Gertrude of Babenberg who was the heir of the Duchy of Austria. This union could have made Ruthenia the status of a formidable ally however, the plan came to little. Daniel further strengthened his relationship to his Russian neighbours by marrying Uatynia with Andrew II, the Prince of Vladimir and Grand Prince of the Rus. Andrew wanted to prove himself in the face of the Golden Horde and was hoping that an alliance with Daniel could help him. however, the Golden Horde severely punishes him.

At the time of his passing away in 1264, Daniel had established the kingdom of Ruthenia the most prosperous and powerful state within Eastern Europe. It stretched across the Carpathians towards the south, and the Pripyat River in north. From the west to the east, it was bordered by Poland and the Dnieper Its area of influence extended into beyond the Black Sea. It was roughly what is now Poland. Daniel's policy had made it stronger against Poland as well as Hungary and protected it, even though it was a token of submission from Tartar anger. The policies also improved the living standards of its inhabitants and helped to boost the economics. Daniel was loved greatly by his fellow citizens, and is still adored by those living in modern Ukraine. The son of Daniel Leo I was as ambitious in his kingdom but he took a completely different path. Leo decided to not fight to the Golden Horde and instead strove to spread to the west. The capital was moved from Ruthenia in Lvov (Lviv) Lviv, which was named in his honor from his late father. Leo is a reference to "lion," and the newly-crowned King of Ruthenia was determined to present this image towards his neighbours. The first goal he had was to conquer Lithuania. The the Grand Duke Mindaugas was killed in 1263 He was succeeded by Vaisvilkas, his younger son Vaisvilkas. A religious figure of religious inclined, Vaisvilkas gave us his domain to live a monastic lifestyle. He gave his crown to Shvarn the brother of his in-laws and the brother of Leo. However, the latter was hoping to take control of Lithuania by himself and became angry enough to have Vaisvillkas executed.

In frustration, Leo turned to the Tartars to reaffirm his loyalty and getting the support by Khan Mengu Timur. Alongside Mongol soldiers, he fought combat against Lithuania however, he was defeated by the Grand Duke Traidenis. Leo was then forced to give up Black Russia, a historic region that was located on the Nemunas River in what is the present-day the central region of Belarus.

The north was defeated, Leo was now seeking to expand to Poland. In 1280, Leo invaded Krakow, the Duchy of Krakow and was under the control of Leszek II who also was the High Duchess of Poland. Nogay Khab, king of the Golden Horde, sent Mongol as well as Russian troops to aid but the war did not succeed. Leo lost at the Battle of Gozlice and was required to leave the country. The campaign against the Hungarians was more successful as he annexed a portion of Carpathia located in northern-east Hungary.

Seven years later, a second assault on Poland took place and was commanded by Nogay and issued invitation to the entire city of Rus for the troops. A total of 30,000 soldiers were gathered to be divided in two groups in accordance with Mongol method of warfare. The first column was led by Talabuga Khan, and Leo I, and consisted of 20000 Tartar along with Russian cavalry. Nogay himself was the commander of the 10,000 Tartar cavalry. Talabuga was able to find the Poles in a state of utter chaos. They had constructed fortresses to defend themselves against the Golden Horde, and an attack on Sandomierz did not succeed. The fortresses of other, smaller ones also were unable to resist, causing Talbuga to break up his forces into a group of raiders. He was not prepared for to see such fortresses in the shape of strong ones or was not prepared for battles of siege. On the 20th of December 1287 the Duke Leszek shocked the Tartars as well as the Ruthenians in Lagow and suffered an defeat of such magnitude that Talabuga was forced to withdraw over the border into Lvov.

When Talabuga began to retreat, Nogay crossed into Poland in a state of confusion, not knowing that the northern war had ended in failure. He fought fortified Cracow but was defeated. As Talabuga and Talabuga, he was a smuggler, but following a raiding team was defeated in the War of Stary Sacz, he likewise went to Volhynia-Galicia where the rage of his enemies was unleashed through pillaging the inhabitants.

It did not end in a total failure so far as Leo was in the matter. He was able to acquire in 1289 Lublin as his border town. Lublin.

The following year, he passed away and left the kingdom of Ruthenia as a powerful country but at a high price. Many thousands of soldiers and massive amount of gold had been spent in the wars he waged against Lithuania. The son Yuri had only 8 years. His brothers, Andrew and Leo II were in the same position. They overturned the foreign policies of Leo I by allied together with the Teutonic knights as well as Poland in opposition to the Lithuanians who were always at war. It was a conflict against the Golden Horde which meant that Ruthenia was at war to live on both sides. The princes both perished without children during battle in 1323 the long-standing lineage of Rurik was dissolved in Ruthenia as the nation's neighbours were ready to take on the leaderless territory.

Chapter 4: The Rise Of Lithuania

In the year Andrew as well as Leo II were dead, Gediminas the Grand Duke of Lithuania was contemplating the possibility of naming his son, the youngest of them Liubatas to be wed to Euphemia who was one of the daughters of King Daniel. But, to make this decision was a risk for Ladislaus I, the King of Poland and also wanted the control of Ruthenia. The war was avoided by an agreement which was that the crown would be presented the crown to Yuri Boleslav, nephew of the late kings. He was a relative of Ladislaus and the ruler of the Polish state of Masovia as well as a cousin of Gediminas the son-in-law of Wenceslaus the Duke of Plock. To seal the arrangement, Yuri married Euphemia, the daughter of Gediminas.

Yuri II commenced his reign in 1323, at the fourteen years old. The king was Masovian and also a Catholic, which made him extremely unpopular among his people. His father Daniel was crowned King by the legate to the pope. However, the religion support of the vast majority of Ruthenians are in Russia as well as Constantinople. The fact that he converted to Orthodoxy was not enough to quell his enemies that were proven by 1338 when he proposed Casimir III of Poland as his successor. The boyars were poisoned by him in 1340, and chose one of them, Dmitry Detko, to take over his place.

The death of Yuri was followed by attacks on Catholics especially Poles who lived in Lvov. King Casimir was able to invade Ruthenia during June 1340 purportedly to defend them, however in reality, it was to bolster his claim on Ruthenia. In August Dmitry accepted the offer and recognized the Polish ruler as his head of state. However, Liubartas of Lithuania had claim to be his own and was able to establish himself as a king in Volhynia which is the northern part of the kingdom. This was his capital being Volodomyr. Dmitry as well as the Poles controlled the south of, Halych. The conflict between Lithuanians as well as the Poles was made worse as the Golden Horde savaged Poland as much as Lublin in winter 1340 to 41. The attack, which was aided with the help of Lithuanian troops, diminished Casimir's power on Volhynia and increased the influence of Liubartas. Charles I of Hungary sent his general William of Drugeth to assist Casimir to fight the Tartars, Lithuanians and Ruthenian boyars. At times, Dmitry successfully played the forces against one another in order to stop the total destruction of his territory. His influence diminished however when he was nearing death, which allowed Casimir as well as Liubartas to agree on a peace which divided the provinces Galicia and Volhynia among them.

The peace was not very long. In 1348 in 1348, the Teutonic Knights, along with the Lithuanians always at war they won a major victory over the Streva River, about 82 kilometers to the west of Vilnius. The Knights claim that 18,000 Lithuanians died, including sixty of them. The Grand Duke, Kestutis, escaped the slaughter, and appealed to Pope Benedict XVI to assist in his Christianization of his country in order to prevent an invasion. But, the Teutonic Order was stricken by the Black Death and in no position to profit from the triumph.

Casimir III was adept at taking advantage of the weaknesses that was his Lithuanian state. In 1349, when Dmitry passed away in 1349, Casimir III was able to exploit the weakness of Lithuanian state. Polish King took over Galicia as well as the western region of Volhynia. The Ruthenians could not resist. Casimir immediately began to work towards integrating the area. The Fiefdoms were granted to Polish powerful people, German as well as Polish merchants were encouraged to settle and Catholic Franciscan as well as the Dominican orders were invited to set up missionaries. The Orthodox structure was preserved and no persecution was enacted.

Lithuania intervened to prevent Casimir from capturing entire Volhynia. The Grand Duke Algirdas faced a battle with both the Poles and Hungarians and was successful by securing a truce 1352 that confirmed his claim to possession of Volhynia. It was not a long time before peace returned however and, by 1353, war recommenced. The treaty was signed in 1366. Lithuania was granted just the eastern part of Volhynia while the remainder together with Galicia and Podolia being transferred to Casimir.

At this point, a mention is required of the eastern neighbours of Lithuania. They were part of the Golden Horde. Golden Horde was experiencing something like a slowdown and was regularly devastated by the civil conflict. However, it was strong within Russia even though the princes of Rus have not yet dared to fight against it, one prince in particular was beginning to take on the role of a leader. Ivan I of Moscow carried an expansionist policy as well as complete devotion towards the Golden Horde in the hope in promoting what was then the status of a minor princely state. In 1328 in 1328, Ivan was granted the title of Grand Duke by the Golden Horde granted him the title as Grand Duke of the Rus as well as the privilege of collecting tributes to the Great Khan in his name. The money Ivan amassed permitted him to buy an area for Muscovy and to make himself essential to the Golden Horde.

In 1362, the Grand Duke Algirdas launched a battle against the Tartars as well as their Russian vassals in the Lower Dnieper and the Bug. The battle was only after the Lithuanians took over Podolia in 1362 that the Horde was able to put up an effective fight. 3 beys (chieftains) came together to confront Algirdas on the shores of Blue Waters, believed to be the present-day village of Torhovystia and a total of 10,000 men. They were referred to as Kutlug, Haci and Demetrius. Algirdas was able to command a bit more Lithuanians as well as Ruthenians possibly as high as 250,000.

The conflict is not widely known and the most reliable account comes taken from Polish historian Maciej Stryjkowski, writing in 1582. According to his account, Algirdas used a semi-circular form of defense against the Tartars and whose arrows did not manage to destroy his heavily armored and shielded soldiers. The crossbowmen were surrounded by them that broke up their lines. They then charged, and defeated the crossbowmen. The victory not only brought Podolia however, but also Kiev and the area that remains today as eastern Ukraine to Crimea in Lithuanian control. The Golden Horde fell to a crushing defeat but was unable to restore the area. However, it maintained its presence with a strong force throughout Crimea and in the southern region of the Dnieper in which it frequently fought the Rus.

The Battle of the Blue Waters caused Lithuania to the forefront of competition with Muscovy as well as seeking supremacy over the entire country of Russia. In 1368 in 1368, prince Dmitry II of Moscow dispossessed Tver's Prince

Michael of Tver and took him to Algirdas who was his brother-in-law. The Prince returned along with the Grand Duke, and an impressive force, accompanied by Moscow's foes Tver as well as Smolensk. The invasion was meticulously designed that the Muscovites were completely shocked. When the invaders exploded and pillaged the city, Dmitry quickly gathered a army that was utterly insufficient to withstand their assault. Dmitry ran back towards the Kremlin fortress, leaving the outer Moscow for the fighters. Algirdas was not in the serious position to attack the fortress and was forced to withdraw within three days devastation.

The year 1370 began the Prince Dmitry was determined to revenge the shame of 1368, took on Tver and Bryansk which were both of which were under the protection of Algirdas. With the help from Algirdas, Michael appealed to Khan

Muhammad Sultan, who was skeptical of the ambitions of Dmitry and appointed Michael as the Grand Prince of Rus. In the same way, Algirdas and Michael laid the city under siege Moscow in the second time, but, this time around prince Dmitry went to the safety within the Kremlin. In the face of Muscovite forces advancing on Moscow, Algirdas reached a peace accord in the month of December. Another invasion took place in the summer of 1372. This time Dmitry was able to stop the Lithuanians getting to Moscow. Through the Treaty of Lyubutsk, Algirdas was able to agree to the demise of Michael of Tver however he remained in the areas he conquered in Russia.

The Battle of Blue Waters and the battles against Muscovy made Lithuania as a major power within Eastern Europe. While Lithuania's Golden Horde continued to be terrorized and exercised formal sovereignty over Muscovy as well as the remaining independent states, it was obvious that it would no longer influence the direction of events that took place in the region. Lithuania and Muscovy eventually became adversaries over the fate of Russia. In the Grand Duke's reign, Lithuania is a pagan and was so to gain the sake of political power, however most of his people comprised Orthodox Ruthenians. In addition, he ruled Kiev, which was the old seat of the Rus and, from 1325 onwards, was also the home of the Orthodox Metropolitan of the entire Rus.

It was 1370 when Casimir from Poland died without sons legitimately born. The Casimir had appointed the nephew of his Louis I of Hungary to succeed to his father, with the caveat that he did not introduce additional taxes or infringe upon the rights of the nobility. Algirdas took advantage temporarily sluggishness that was the Polish government in order to take over the west of Volhynia. The war among Volhynia and Poland was not rekindled at a high level until 1376 in which time the Lithuanians attacked Poland up to Cracow. Louis tried to counterattack with some results, but the battle about Volhynia quickly became a larger battle that involved Lithuania, Poland, Hungary as well as Poland, Hungary as well as the Teutonic Order.

In 1377, the Grand Duke Algirdas passed away and was replaced by the son of his Jogaila. The constant threat from the Teutonic Knights was especially strong in the period of 1377 and Jogaila was contemplating changing his religion to Christianity to put an end to the Teutonic campaign. The conversion to Orthodoxy will not solve the issue, as the Knights were adamant about the diasporic

Russians nearly as unpalatable like the heathen Lithuanians. The Russians sought to form a marriage union with the Poles and was able to propose marriage Jadwiga her daughter Louis I of Hungary and his successor in 1384. Jadwiga was 11 years older and was highly fragile. Her marriage was urgently required to prevent the possibility of civil war. Many of the Polish nobles wanted a marriage with Jogaila that would ensure peace at the border of Poland's east as well as strengthen Poland against it being a victim of the Teutonic Order. Jogaila swears solemnly to be baptized as a Catholic and also to Christianize his country.

Jagiello the Grand Duke will first, along with the rest of his brothers who are not yet Baptized and also with his family members, nobles, as well as land-owners both large and small, who live within his land, sincerely look for and wish to be baptized into the Catholic belief that is the Holy Roman Church. Although many emperors and princes endeavored to the goal, they achieved the smallest amount despite their arduous efforts. However, God almighty has reserved the honor to your personal sovereign power. [11]

Jadwiga and Jogaila were wed on the 18th of February 1366. The couple was given the new title Ladislaus. On March 4, he became the King of Poland as the second person in the history of this title, and was reigning alongside his wife. Poland and Lithuania were separate states that shared the same monarchs, and were subject to their own law and practices. However, Ladislaus was obliged to swear that he would forever join his territories in Lithuania in addition to Ruthenia in the throne of the Kingdom of Poland.'[12The alliance created the biggest empire of its kind in Europe which extended across

Germany in the west all the way to the Dnieper to the east as well as north and south from the Carpathian Mountains, which today is Latvia in north.

Jogaila's change of heart did not protect Lithuania from the Knights that claimed they were right, and perhaps his decision to convert was not sincere. The Knights also suggested that the people in general would not be willing to surrender their old beliefs as well as the ancient faith remained in place for a long time. It was, however, hypocritical to the extreme due to the gruesome lengths to which they went to forcefully convert Prussians as well as Livonians. Actually, the Teutonic Order required Lithuania to become a heathen state for the sake of attracting many knights. Without a foe to fight or new territories to acclimatize, the Order could be extinct.

The second obstacle came from Jogaila's older brother Vytautas. He was attempting to become Grand Duke following the demise of his father Algirdas and was not hesitant to make use of to join the Teutonic Order to do so. He was baptized as a Catholic in order to win their approval and he later sat down with Jogaila once he realized the support for his uncle was not enough. However, he did not abandon the possibility of becoming Grand Duke. And when Ladislaus (Jogaila) named his brother Skirgaila as the regent of Lithuania instead of himself, He was angry. Skirgaila did not enjoy the approval of Lithuanian people, and a few Lithuanian dukes was in support of Vytautas.

Vytautas tried to take over Vilnius The capital city in Lithuania that was held by Polish forces. The plan was devised that an armed escort bringing provisions and food to Vilnius was to take over the garrison.

However, the plan was found. Vytautas was then the leader of a group of nobles for his fellow knights, the Teutonic Knights, and, on the 26th of May 1390, he signed the Treaty of Konigsberg that gave Samogitia (north-western Lithuania) in exchange for assistance.

Chapter 5: The Knights Engaged In The War Against

Vytautas in the name of a crusade in that sense, it attracted many the mercenaries of Western Europe, including the potential Henry IV of England, the Earl of Derby and Jean Le Maingre Marshal of France. The group began with various small battles including pillaging and burning Ladislaus fortresses located in Lithuania however, over time, they turned their efforts on capturing Georgenburg (Jubarkas) located in the Samogitia region. The fortress was too powerful and along together with Vytautas and his troops made up of Lithuanians Ruthenians fighting, they struck Vilnius rather than Vilnius.

The fortress that was the most formidable of the Lithuanians actually an island located along the banks of the Neris River, completely surrounded by water, and protected by three impressive castles. The

Grand of Rothenstsein von Rothenstsein succeeded in taking one of the citadels following intense fighting and was then forced to surrender within five weeks, in the month of the month of October in 1390. They were hindered with a shortage of provisions as well as western crusaders returning their home towns. The Knights were forced to go back to Prussia in search of a alternative to von Rothenstein, who had lost his life in the battle.

The battle of Vilnius was an expensive event. The city's ruin was wiped out as well as many nobles on both sides died. Both sides had not gained an advantage in strategic terms against each other and, consequently, no significant actions were taken during all of. The Teutonic Order being dominated by the selection of the new Grand Master, Vytautas searched for new allies. 21 January 1391, he got married to Sophia, his child Sophia and

Vasily I, the Grand Duke of Muscovy. Vasily was following the policy of his predecessors, which was expansion, at the expense of neighbouring Russian princes. He was also to the risk of angering his Golden Horde. The alliance with Vytautas will strengthen his hands in negotiations in dealings with the Horde. However, the agreement was not as strong it was also a source of danger for Vasily took advantage of it to gain Russian land while contributing nothing to the military effort. But Vytautas may be, at the least, feel certain of the friendship between Muscovy and Russia.

In 1391, the fall of the newly appointed Grand Master of the Teutonic Order, Konrad von Wallenrode prepared to launch a fresh campaign against Vilnius However, it could not move beyond the sacking of towns and villages around. Both sides appeared to have any distinct advantages. Both Lithuanian as well as Polish nobles wished to bring peace to end the war however Ladislaus and Vytautas could be persuaded into a compromise. The king was willing to recognise Vytautas as the Grand Duke, if Vytautas, in turn accepted him as his lord. Skirgaila was promised compensation by the appointment of a governor in Kiev at the time, which was the town was of little significance. The Teutonic Knights were disappointed and maintained their attacks against Lithuanian land until being tempered through the surrender of Samogitia in the month of October 1398.

Grand Duke Vytautas called "the Great" ruled until the year 1430, when he died. His big dream was to be the ruler of all of Rus, so he started to consolidate his authority over the Ruthenian territory he had already owned. He sacked members who were part of the royal clan, who controlled the principalities. Prince Volodomir from Kiev was one of the targets. He was the descendant of Algirdas the prince was an independent monarch. He minted himself coins, as well as paying respect towards the Golden Horde but without Vytautus the consent of. In 1394 The Grand Duke came into his Principality of Kiev and turned over Volodomir without resistance. In relation to the connection with Poland the plan was to renounce it once his defeat of the Tartars.

Then, Vytautas made alliances with Russian states that were wary of Muscovite expansion. This angered His father-in-law Vasily I. He put up fortifications to stop his Golden Horde in the south and east. Then, when, in 1395 Khan Tokhtamysh showed up at the Lithuanian court to seek assistance to restore the throne, he saw an chance. Tokhtamysh was exiled by his position in the Golden Horde by his rival Timur Qutluq, backed by Timur the Lame, who was the founder of the legendary Timurid Empire. Tokhtamysh said he would renounce his claim to supreme suzerainty on Ruthenia to gain assistance. The Grand Duke then began creating an army of his extensive empire. He gathered Lithuanians, Ruthenians (remember, Ruthenian is the Western term used to describe Russian), Poles, Moldavians, and Wallachians. The Teutonic Knights provided a tiny strength and Tokhtamysh enjoyed the support to a few Tartars.

The offensive's first phase was launched in 1397. It spanned to Crimea. The war took thousands of Tartar captives, who were later relocated to Lithuania. They are still there today. In 1398, another attack spanned the Don however, the capital of the Golden Horde was at Sarai located on the Volga River, several hundred miles further to the to the east. They established an army base in Kiev as well, and Vytautas requested the Pope Boniface IX to call for an offensive against the Tartars. The pope agreed, although the ensuing crusade could not draw large amounts of tourists, it established Lithuania's credibility as an independent Catholic country that did not require of Christianization by itself.

In 1399, during the summer In 1399, the Christian forces were ready to fight the Horde. After leaving Kiev the force moved to the south-east across the Dnieper and on the 5th of 5 August, it spotted the remains of a Tartar army along the Vorskla river near Poltava about 140 km from the west of Kharkov. It was made up of 90,000 troops and was led by Khan Timur Qutluq as well as Edigu. The Grand Duke Vytautas was in charge of 38,000 soldiers with 50 princes. They included Tokhtamysh as well as the princes of Polotsk and Bryansk which were both Russian Principalities that were that were administered by members of the Lithuanian royal family. Even though they were smaller in numbers however, they had better equipment and had a large arsenal of gunspowder artillery. As a result they were able to defend themselves. Timur traditionally gave peace as a token of respect, Vytautas demanded that he surrender to him. A truce was enacted for three days in order to permit each side to set up their armies, but, in reality, they were merely to provide the reinforcements time to get to Timur. Vytautas was also thankful for this time period, as the next day he started building a defense complex. The structure consisted of a band of wagons that were plated with wooden shields, and operated by handgunners and archers and cannon as well as other artillery. Mobile fortifications like this were Impregnable to cavalry that was heavy. The Hussites from

Bohemia were famous by the end of the 15th century. As were European settlements of North America in the 19th century.

Hostilities erupted on August 12 and ended on August 12, with Timur surrounding the Lithuanian fort and pouring the fort with archers. The majority of them hid themselves within the wooden shields, or looked away from their shields without a thought. Timur was wise to not take on an attack which is why he resorted an old Mongol strategy - a fake retreat. The fort was attacked by Tartars and quickly turned around and left. This action must have been well-known to the Rus as well as the Lithuanians especially that it's quite surprising that Vytautas broken the defenses to chase the Tartars. Maybe Vytautas did not have any experience combating the Horde however Tokhtamysh was probably warning him.

When the defensive circle was cracked and Vytautas was on the move the Tartars appeared out of the woods surrounding and gullies, and came on the Lithuanian troops. The surprise enemy battled bravely for a few minutes, but then began to destroy. Vytautas ran back in a hurry to rescue his soldiers, who were now being in the pursuit of Tartars who made a pretense to leave. In the middle of 2 divisions in the Horde He fought to get away, but only achieved it through his the courage of his efforts. The two cousins Dmitry and Andrew didn't fall, but they did together with the prince Stephen of Moldavia along with 17 noblemen. The majority of the army was demolished as of now nothing that could stop the Horde burning down the towns and villages towns in Ruthenia.

The principal objective of the victors, the Tartars was to kill or the capture of

Tokhtamysh and the destroyed Ukraine following. They occupied Kiev and demanded the ransom of its own to prevent the dreadful fate of cities in other countries that opposed to the Golden Horde. The search for Tokhtamysh went on for 8 years, causing the immense misery of the principality of Kiev. The hunt ended when he was assassinated in 1407.

The catastrophe in Vorskla put an end to any chance of Vytautas being the ruler of the entire Rus. This caused unrest among those who were his Orthodox Ruthenian subjects and emboldened Muscovy. Additionally, he was required be drawn close to Poland and affirm his loyalty to Ladislaus. The Horde has shown that it is not just a stalemate, and Tartar forces continued to destroy Ukraine as well as Muscovy until the end of in the early 16th century. The last incursions to Ukraine by the forces of Crimea didn't end until 18th century.

If Vytautas defeated during the Battle of the Vorskla, it's possible that Lithuania rather than Muscovy could have brought together with the Russian peoples. In the end, Lithuania and Western Ruthenia were relegated toward Poland and to the Catholic West and further defined the gap in culture in Ruthenia as well as Muscovy. It isn't to suggest that Lithuania is no longer an important force within Eastern Europe. The most significant achievement of Vytautas was, in all likelihood, the destruction of the Teutonic Order in the Battle of Grunwald, or Tannenberg the 1410 battle. Along with Poland and Poland, the Lithuanians suffered such a devastating loss against the Knights that they did not come back after which they were no longer able from being an enemy. Following Grunwald, Vytautas needed only to gaze east, towards Muscovy and to the Golden Horde.

Vytautas was killed in 1430 which made the Lithuanian empire as the biggest in Europe. Despite the loss in Vorskla the Lithuanian empire was comparatively secured, with Muscovy as well as the Golden Horde not able to take it over. It was the Grand Prince who ruled Moscow was principally involved in expanding his territory into other principalities as well as maintaining a tense relationship with the Tartars which were, in fact, his lord. The death of Vytautas the Great brought the empire into another crises and an ensuing civil conflict. The position of Grand Duke was a choice, but it required the consent of the King of Poland which, as of 1430, still ruled as Ladislaus (Jogaila). Vytautas his cousin Svritrigaila the son of the Grand Duke Algirdas believed that he was the ideal candidate and to secure approval from his fellow Orthodox Ruthenian boyars, promised to give them the same status as Catholic Lords.

Svritrigaila was subsequently elected Grand Duke to anger of the Polish nobility who insisted to ensure that the rights and privileges of Ladislaus be respected. Actually, Ladislaus was present in Vilnius in the same time to mourn the death of Vytautas who was compelled to accept the presidency. Although he was not arrested The king was, however, actually held hostage to the ransom. As he was negotiating with the new government over the future relations with Poland and Lithuania Unrest was raging within Volhynia as well as Podolia and Podolia, both of which according to the provisions of a treaty that was signed by Ladislaus as well as Vytautas were to be returned into that of the Polish crown. Polish forces entered Podolia and Svritrigaila was able to capture Ladislaus but only let him go Ladislaus after he agreed to hand over Podolia the state of Lithuania.

Additionally, Zbigniew Olesnicki, Archbishop of Cracow and the top magnate of Poland was the one who called a meeting of the Polish nobility in Sandomierz that made the decision to renounce Podolia in nullity and unenforceable and requested that Svritrigaila honor Ladislaus. Svritrigaila was able to respond by rejecting the association with Poland. He sought out allies. The most notable was Sigismund, Holy Roman Emperor and King of Hungary He contacted Sigismund, the Holy Roman Emperor and King of Hungary to make him the King of Lithuania. However, there was a doubt as to what kind of support Sigismund could offer, since it was at that time the king was preoccupied by three important matters: his coronation in Rome as well as the ecumenical conference of the Catholic Church in Florence and also the Hussite heresy that was sweeping through Bohemia. In the end, it was clear that Teutonic Knights were more dependable as allies because - being weak, they were resentful of the chance to take revenge for Grunwald. After a few initial victories however, the Order was crushed by Polish knights in the battle of Dabki in the in the southern part of Danzig (Gdansk) on 13 September 1431. Then, in September 1431 13th, 1431, it was reported that the Teutonic Order and Lithuania had reached a two-year agreement with Ladislaus.

In April 1432 Ladislaus proposed to officially recognize Svritrigaila in exchange for consent, but the king did not accept. A few months later the nobles took the group and their entourage while they were on their way to Grodno. He was able to escape to Polotsk however his partner Anna of Tver remains captive. The conspirators later selected Sigismund Kestutatis as Duke of Navahradak as well as Starodub, the Grand Duke opposing Svritigailia. Veteran from Vorskla and Grunwald He was an advocate of Svritrigaila and was subsequently persuaded by a group comprised of Lithuanian, Polish and Ruthenian nobles to agree. In the Union of Grodno, he recognized Ladislaus to be "our lord and senior brother" and himself as the Grand Duke (Supremus princeps) in tempora vitae (for all of the time in his existence). This means that the Grand Duke could not transfer the title at his demise. This agreement was not other than the one that was agreed upon by Vytautas however, it was different in the sense that following the death of Sigismund, Lithuania would revert to the Polish crown. Sigismund was also obliged to give

Podolia as well as parts of Volhynia to Poland to the condition that the entire area would be transferred to Poland following his death.

Bishop Olesnicki declared Sigismund Grand Prince of Grodno which is in the region that is today Belarus. In order to gain the trust by his fellow Orthodox Ruthenian boyars, Sigismund recognized their legal rights like Svritrigaila did. Then he left Vilnius and exiled Svritrigaila and reestablished his position in Polotsk within modern Belarus located 255 km north-east of. The Lithuanian empire was divided between the two dukes competing for supremacy. The Lithuanian Core lands as well as Minsk province Minsk stood behind Sigismund but the vast majority of Ruthenian territories, which includes Kiev, the Principality of Kiev was in support of Svritrigaila.

In the winter of 1432, Svritrigaila set out from Polotsk along with 40000 Russians as well as Tartars. They were led by Sayid Ahmad I, Khan of the Golden Horde, who benefited from the civil war that erupted during the Lithuanian empire. The objective of the army was Vilnius as well, and to counter, Sigismund was able to gather a group of 20.000 Samogitians as well as Masurians (inhabitants of the southern part of Prussia). They met at Ashmiany near Grodno in the middle of Grodno, and the fight was fought all morning. Initially, Svritrigaila drove Sigismund's forces about five kilometers away from Grodno however in the afternoon they were able to counterattack. At night, Svritrigaila was on the move in the air, and saw the death of 10,000 of his soldiers and 4000 captured.

Chapter 6: Sigismund Was A Victim Of Huge Losses

The war raged on intermittently and intermittently for the next three years. In 1435, during the summer, Svritrigaila initiated a series of attacks across Lithuania from the eastern part of Ruthenia and the Teutonic Knights of Livonia joined in, as did their commander, Franco Kerskorfff. The incursions were set to be capped off by a decisive battle which was to ultimately destroy Sigismund. Svritrigaila created a troop of 11,000 soldiers for the mission comprised of Ruthenians who were from Polotsk, Volhynia, Kiev, Vitebsk and Smolensk, Knights of the Livonian Order (a branch of the Teutonic Knights) and around 500 Tartars from the Golden Horde. It's possible that a few Bohemian Hussite mercenaries fought with the mercenaries, since Svritigaila's son, Sigismund Korybut, was the leader of. Korybut was one of the leaders of the Hussites that, at one moment, had received an award of the crown in Bohemia. Hussite militias were mostly infantry that were adept at defense tactics, and skilled in making use of guns, that were beginning to play a major function in war. Grand Duke Sigismund brought together about 9,500 soldiers in order to take on the danger. Michael, his son Michael was in charge of the Lithuanians and Jakob Kobylanski, a Polish nobleman who was a former courtier of the Grand Duke Vytautas was in charge of 4000 Polish forces.

His plan was to set out from Vitebsk and then march 250 kilometers to the west, and then Braslaw which was where he'd be joined by the Livonians following which he was to march about 200 km south-west towards Vilnius and Trakai, which were the main cities within Sigismund. The terrain between was usually marshy with numerous streams and lakes that impeded moving. Both armies met around 78 kilometres north-west Vilnius in a town called Wilkomierz (Polish for the area that is now Ukmerge). The town was located at the confluence between the Vilkmerge and Sventoji Rivers, Wilkomierz was not a stranger to battle. The city had been targeted by Teutonic Knights five times since 1333. In the most recent attack that took place in 1391, it was burned to the ground despite the fact that it was a convert to Catholic Christianity.

The army was unable to deploy because of a swampy bed and lake between them. It wasn't until two days later on September 1st on the 1st, when Sigismund identified a perfect occasion. The force of Svritigaila's maneuvering was cut into a rivulet after it hit. Svritrigaila was shocked and incapable of forming defensive positions. The next phase was more of war than a massacre. In a few minutes of brutal battle that included those of the Ruthenians, Livonians, Bohemians and Tartars started to fall. A lot of them, engulfed in swamps, were killed. Some threw themselves in the waters and sank to death. The victims included Korskorff, Korybut and Sigismund de Rota who was the envoy to the Holy Roman Emperor. The reserve of Svritigaila, who arrived to late, was compelled to sign a surrender.

The survivors were brutally chased throughout the marshes for 15 days. Svritrigaila fled, and then went back to Polotsk with only 30 of his men. The gang quickly abandoned the rebel. The loss was far too great even for Teutonic as well as the Livonian Knights. Following Grunwald this defeat proved far too great for the fragile Order to take on, so they quickly made peace by acknowledging Sigismund as well as Polish sovereignty over

Lithuania. They firmly stated to it was the Grand Duchy was a Christian state, and would never become the focus of an armed campaign. Svritrigaila did not agree to give up his claim to the king, and in 1437, suggested to Sigismund to surrender his rights for Volhynia as well as the Principality of Kiev. The Polish Nobles' assembly refused to approve of the plan so Svritrigaila left for Poland.

In 1440, the Grand Duke Sigismund was killed by a group of nobles that were supportive of Svritrigaila. The prince who was exiled sought to be crowned, however, his attempt failed. Council of Nobles elected the younger child of Ladislaus II, Casimir. Ladislaus was dead in 1434 and the new king's brother, Casimir's Ladislaus III was dismayed over the fact that Lithuanians did not respect the promise Sigismund signed which was following his demise, the crown would go back to the monarch of Poland. In 1447 The Grand Duke was chosen to succeed his brother Casimir IV.

The year 1452 was the time that Svritrigaila was killed in 1452 at Lutsk which is located in the present northwestern Ukraine. His death was the beginning of Ruthenian independence in the Grand Duchy of Lithuania. If Svritrigaila had been successful in winning over Sigismund the king would have established the state of the southern part of Russia instead of Lithuania. However, the pro-Polish government in Vilnius was able to weaken the Ruthenians. Casimir was savagely resisted through the prince Olelko Volodymyrovich of Kiev, the grandson of the Grand Duke Algirdas. He was the husband of Anastasia and was the niece of Great Prince Vasily I of Moscow. Olelko was a patron of his Ukrainian Orthodox Church, and he vigorously stood up for the sovereignty of Kiev. He established political connections with Lithuania's Chancellor Lithuania, Jonas Gostautas, who sought to exile the Poles from government in the Grand Duchy. In 1456, Gostautas attempted to take down Casimir and succeed him as Grand Duke with the son of Olelko Semen which was tied to his own daughter Maria. However, the plan failed and in 1471, Casimir removed the principality of Kiev and made voivodes (governors) to replace the princes.

The Olelko family Olelko maintained a significant influence through its home at Slutsk-Kapyl, which is now Belarus. The year 1481 was the time Michael was a son of Semen led a gang to murder Casimir and take over the Grand Duchy. The plot was exposed before conspirators were able to take action to take action, which was the reason Michael got killed. After that, the family did not hold any land in Kiev's Voivodeship of Kiev however, they continued to manage land in Belarus and help the administration of Lithuania.

The Ukrainian struggle for freedom from Vilnius was a part of a larger conflict within the Crimea Peninsula, lands below the Dnieper and to the east of the Don. The inhabitants of this region split from the Golden Horde and called themselves the Great Horde, better known as the Crimean Khanate. Their leader in 1441, Haci Gray, had achieved the feat of removing the golden Horde and had established his palace at Qirq Yur (now Bagcasaray). After his death, his children fought for the throne. The dispute was resolved with the help of Ottoman Turks, who had quickly become the dominant power throughout the Middle East and the Balkans. The Great Horde came to be an imperial ally of the Ottoman Sultans and was aided with their immense capabilities, human resources and military strength. Aided by the Ottomans The Crimean Tartars began to raid and pillaging the territories of the Rus and in particular, the land that were part of the Ukrainian Steppe, known then as The Wild Fields. Their primary target was Christians who were able to be sold and captured to slaves at the market in the Ottoman Empire. As with the Ottomans however, the Tartars were Christians They were also Christians, as was the case with the Ottomans, and Islamic law allowed only the slavery of non-Muslims. The estimates suggest that up to 1,000,000 Christians in Poland or Lithuania were enslaved between 1474 and 1694 [14], although the final attacks did not cease until 1769.

The year 1483 was when Khan Menli II Giray took over Kiev. Kiev as well as Crimean Tartars re-attacked in 1496, and again in 1500. They did not care about the acquisition of territory but more in booty and slaves, in addition to keeping their enemies at bay. Vilnius was far enough away to aid, so all the Voivode from Kiev did was to fortify the best way possible. As soon as the alarm went off and the people of small towns and villages were forced to flee the fortress wall of fortresses. However, this is not to suggest that the Poles as well as the Lithuanians were unable to compete with the Tartar forces. Outnumbered by a large margin, they beat them in Kletsk (1506) in 1506) and Wisniowiec (1512). But, for the major portion, the raids were not able to be stopped, which meant that they were unable to stop them, and the Wild Fields were kept constantly in a state of weakness and political paralysis. At one time, a thriving, and or even dominant participant in the affairs of the Grand Duchy, the Ukraine was reduced to the status of a backwater political entity dependent on Lithuania as well as Poland.

In the reign of Casimir IV as well as his successors under Casimir IV and his successors, Casimir IV and his successors, the Grand Duchy of Lithuania and the Kingdom of Poland continued to remain separate entities, each having its own law as well as nobility, military and laws. The union of the two was personal which means that they were ruled by the common monarch. The Lithuanian nobles were able to enjoy their privileges, including having the power to choose the grand Duke. In theory, they could pick a monarch who wasn't the monarch of Poland this possibility caused a tense situation for Poland's crown. Polish crown. The dissolution of two crowns was an extremely possible scenario after King Sigismund II recognized that after three marriages, he was likely to pass away without a successor. With a poor state of health, he called the nobles in Poland as well as Lithuania to discuss a permanent and indefinite union of Poland and Lithuania. Grand Duchy whereby the two crowns would merge.

It is believed that the Lithuanian nobles were not willing to sign a treaty because the Polish nobles were vastly superior to those from Lithuania. But they relied upon them during a battle against Muscovy in the battle of Livonia and, later then became a vassal of Grand Duchy. Ivan IV, 'The Terrible Ivan IV', declared himself to be the first tsar or emperor over the entire Rus of 1547 and had taken off the rule from the Golden Horde. Lithuania was fighting to save its existence as Ivan declared his claim on all Ruthenian territories.

In 1569 1569, The Sejm which is also called the Parliament of Poland was convened in

Lublin to welcome a group composed of Lithuanian nobles in order to discuss an agreement for a union. The Poles were seeking the right to establish themselves in the lands of the Lithuanian Crown. The idea was not a favorite among the majority of the Lithuanians and they retreated from the country in protest. The Ruthenian boyars were largely for joining the Union, as they believed it was a way to gain political independence from Vilnius and also economic benefits. Additionally, Poland was better able to protect the Ruthenian nobles against Muscovy. In the event that Sigismund unilaterally added Ruthenia in Poland Polish crown, boys were generally in favor of Polish rule. This brave move stripped Lithuania from a large portion of its economic and military influence, and its nobles went back to Lublin and embraced joining the two crowns. In the words in the Union of Lublin, "The Kingdom of Poland and the

Grand Duchy of Lithuania are an unifying and homogenous entity and also a uniform Commonwealth that grew and was merged into a single nation of two nations and states. One leader, one head and a common king must be the supreme ruler of this joint nation. The king will be chosen by jointly voted votes by both the Poles as well as the Lithuanians as well as be sworn by the people of Poland after which he will be anointed, crowned and presented to Poland and the Kingdom of Poland in Krakow. In accordance with the rights of the King Aleksander (a former king, and Grand Duke], absence of any party could hinder the process of deciding, since each estate of Poland and the Grand Duchy of Lithuania Crown of Poland and the Grand Duchy of Lithuania are required to be called to vote. The election as well as the inauguration of the Grand Duke of Lithuania that was previously a place in Lithuania will be cancelled. No resemblance or sign of this should be seen later on, and could lead to or be a basis to the grand opening by the Grand Duke of Lithuania. In addition, as that of the Grand Duchy of Lithuania and its official titles remain, at the coronation ceremony and during the elections, the ruler is expected to be declared as King of Poland and Grand Duke of Lithuania, Ruthenia, Prussia, Masovia, Samogitia, Kiev, Volhynia, Podlachia [Podolia] as well as Livonia."[15[15]

Following the union, Polish nobles moved to the secluded Wild Fields. They brought the Polish language as well as Catholicism. A large portion of the Ruthenian nobles adopted the Polish religious and language, believing that they were paths to the economic and social advantages. The nobles of the upper class generally accepted Catholicism as well as those who were not desired the status the polonization gave them. A majority people in people in Ruthenian Orthodox Church acknowledged the supremacy that was the Pope and was a part of with the Catholic Church. It was the Union of Brest (1596) brought the Orthodox Ruthenian churches into communion with Rome was not a forced move however, it did at times, provoke a rebellion among the poor. However, in the vast majority it was recognized as a good thing.

Poland took over the mantle as protector and ruler of the Rus the Rus, a position that was challenged by the leader of Muscovy who was now referred to as the Tsar of All Rus. "Tsar" is the Slavic term for Caesar and the kings of Russia took the title after the passing of the final Roman emperor at Constantinople at the time of 1453. In exchange, they were granted the defense that was provided by the Orthodox Church against the attacks from the corruption-ridden Western Church that was founded in Rome. For the tsars the unified state of all Rus under their control was a sacred duty as a crusade in order to protect them from Catholicism. The the cleric Philotheus of Pskov sent a letter to his ruler Vasily III Moscow:

Be aware, a lover of God and Christ and Christ, that the majority of Christian empires are coming to an end, and have been joined in the single kingdom of our sovereign, as per the Bibles of prophecy. And this will be the Russian empire, since two Romes are gone, another is standing, but four more will never exist. [16]

It's easy to recognize that there is a parallel in the relationship with Russia and Ruthenia in the aftermath of the Union of Lublin with that between the Russian Federation and Ukraine today. The tsars viewed Kiev as their territory by the divine right of their country, but they were corrupted due to those who were Polish and their religious. The same is true for Putin. Putin views Ukraine as an integral part of Russia which has been affected and corrupted by West as well as that Russia's goal is in order to bring it back to its home country and to preserve the country.

The historical background of historically, the Ukraine region was looking to the west for a long time prior to the Polish annexed. Cultural differences between eastern and western Rus started with the Mongol invasion. The princes of Galicia and Volhynia asked for help from Poles in their fight against the Tartars while the rest of Rus was ruled by. Then, it gradually taken over by The Grand Duchy of Lithuania which at one point seemed to be the one to unite all of Rus.

For a brief overview of the state of Ruthenia following Ruthenia's status following the Union of Lublin: the ancient areas that comprised Volhynia, Podolia and Kiev which are which are now included in Ukraine are included in the Polish crown and were, effectively, Polish colonies. The eastern bank of Dnieper River was ruled by the Crimean Khanate as well as, to the west, by was the Ottoman Empire. The Tsardom in Russia has defeated the Golden Horde, threatened Kiev from to the west. In the second half in the sixteenth century an additional power came into the basins of Dnieper and the Don. The Cossacks were independent nomads, not Ruthenian or Russian They were to play a significant role in the cultural and historical growth of the region that became the present Ukraine. Ukraine.

Chapter 7: Background And Context

Relationships with Ukraine and Russia are a lengthy and complex history that includes times of unity in politics as well as submission and tension. In a tangled web of economic, cultural as well as demographic connections towards both the Russian Empire and subsequently the Soviet Union, Ukraine was in the past a part of both. Ukraine was declared independent in the year 1991 in the aftermath of the demise of the Soviet Union. There were challenges, including the restructuring of its economy along with political instability as well as attempts to build democratic institutions were a part of the nation's independence. There has been conflict between pro-European as well as pro-Russian elements in Ukraine's politics.

Different regions in Ukraine differ in their political orientations and the regions in western Ukraine typically favoring closer ties to Europe and the east and southern regions enjoy stronger historic, cultural and economic connections to Russia. The end of 2013 saw massive protests took place within Kyiv's Maidan Nezalezhnosti (Independence Square) also popularly referred to as the Euromaidan protests. These protests began due to the government's decision delay the sign-off of an associate arrangement with European Union, but they eventually grew to include demand for democratic reforms as well as the end of corruption. There was a strong pro-Russia sentiment within the east Ukrainian region that included Donetsk and Luhansk and Luhansk, with tensions increased by the addition of Crimea as well as political changes that took place in Kiev. Separatists who favored closer relations with Russia declared their independence and started a war against Ukrainian authorities. Ukrainian government. Russia has been accused of aiding the rebels of separatists in Eastern Ukraine militarily, providing soldiers, arming them as well as paying them.

In spite of its claims, evidence and reports indicate that Russia has provided significant support to rebel forces. Russo-Ukrainian War deaths, displaced population, destruction of infrastructure and the loss of resources are but a handful of the grave human consequences.

Security concerns in the region and stability are also triggered through the war, and potential consequences for other countries. Geopolitical conditions have also been affected by NATO's increasing participation within Eastern Europe and efforts to negotiate a settlement diplomatically at a global level. Despite sporadic cease-fires as well as ongoing diplomatic efforts to reach an agreement that is permanent however, the conflict hasn't ever been concluded.

The situation is still evolving It's not clear how to reach peace and end the issue.

Objectives And Scope

Particularly in the pro-Russian areas in Donetsk and Luhansk located in eastern Ukraine, Russia sought to maintain or grow its presence there. Stopping NATO from GrowingAs the expansion of NATO was perceived as a threat to Russia as a threat to its security as well as its region of influence, it sought to block Ukraine from gaining membership. Protecting the Russian-speaking population: Russian officials asserted that they intervened in defense of the rights and well-being of Russian-speaking people in the country particularly those living in Crimea and in the Donbass region. The principal motives of Ukraine were to protect its territorial integrity, and to regain control over its Donetsk and Luhansk regions which were in the hands of rebels. To counter Russian pressure and aggression, Ukraine determined to assert its sovereignty and independence. The Ukrainian administration tried to implement democratic reforms in the country, combat corruption as well as acquaint itself with European rules and regulations. The military's operations were routine and sporadic were employed in the course of war. Ukrainian Government forces, supported by battalions of volunteers, were engaged in combat with separatists from Russia. groups in the eastern part of Ukraine. There were allegations of Russian military intervention, including the presence of Russian military personnel and equipment. The fighting was focused on three regions: Crimea, Donetsk, and Luhansk. Russia has annexed Crimea in 2014 and fighting in the eastern part of

Ukraine was focused on taking the control of areas occupied by separatists. There were thousands of casualties as well as massive evictions of civilians destruction of infrastructure as well as a lack of necessities within the affected areas The war caused an incredibly devastating humanitarian catastrophe. In order to end the war peacefully the various talks and initiatives took place. International organisations like that of United Nations and the Organization for Security and Cooperation in Europe (OSCE) in addition to in addition to individual nations acting as mediators were participants in the efforts.

Russia has declared that it would like to disarm Ukraine since it views the country as a security risk. It could be referring to

Gymnasium Alexandrinum: school in Ukraine

disarming the Ukrainian military, or larger, like the destruction of the military industrial complex of Ukraine. Russia is also accusing Ukraine as the country's first Nazi state and claims it wants in order to "denazify" the nation. This could include removing any Nazi images and ideologies out of Ukraine and could include removing any pro-Western political leaders or bureaucrats off the job. Additionally, Russia has declared its desire to "liberate" the pro-Russian separatist-controlled Donbas area of Ukraine. This could include an annexation of the Donbass region or involve a less dramatic measure such as establishing a puppet government in the Donbass region. The scope of the war has altered. Initially, the focus was on targets for military use, Russia has since started attack on civilian infrastructure. A large number of citizens are forced out of their homes due to the attack and a lot of people have been killed. The war could reach a peaceful resolution through negotiation or mediation, however it may persist for a few months or perhaps even for several years. The outcome of the war could have an enormous impact on the direction of Russia, Ukraine, and all of the globe.

Historical Background Of The War

The story of the Russo-Ukrainian War, which started in 2014, is complex and intricate, with a long history that spans millennia. Knowing the historical context will help us comprehend the root causes and dynamics behind the conflict. Medieval as well as Early Modern Period: Kyivan Rus was a state in the medieval period which was founded in the 9th century, was formerly part of the region that is now today's Ukraine. Kyivan Rus had strong political and cultural connections to adjacent Baltic as well as Slavic nations. Kyivan Rus was conquered by the Mongols at the end of the 13th century and they were in charge for several centuries following that. The cultural and political growth was greatly affected by the time of slavery.

Cossack Hetmanate And Commonwealth Of Poland And Lithuania:

The Cossacks were a semi-nomadic army class, led numerous uprisings against the authority of Polish-Lithuanian during the seventeenth century. The purpose of these uprisings was to secure an independent state and to defend those rights that were a part of community. Orthodox Christian community. The Cossack Hetmanate, which is a partly self-governing nation that has its capital located in Ukraine was created in the 19th century by Cossacks. The Hetmanate was a key player of Eastern European politics throughout its period of relative freedom as well as political turmoil.

The partition of Poland and Russian Imperial Rule: In the latter half of 18th century Austria-Hungary, Prussia, and the Russian Empire each claimed a part of Ukraine. A large portion of Ukrainian area was seized by Russia.

The Russification Policy: When Ukraine was controlled by Russia There were many attempts to suppress Ukrainian tradition and language as well as encouraging Russian influence.

Repression and Famine Afflicted on the Ukrainian populace was subject to brutal repression as well as massive famines such as the devastating Holodomor during the 1930s. in 1922 Ukraine became known then as the Ukrainian Soviet Socialist Republic, was recognized in the Republics of the Soviet Union.

World War II: The Nazi invasion and occupation of Ukraine has had an enormous impact on the nation, leading to massive destruction, mass killing and forced migrations. As part of the efforts of the Soviet Union to defeat Nazi Germany, Ukraine was an important participant.

Independence and The Decline Of the Soviet Union: As the Soviet Union started to fall to pieces in the 1980s in the 1990s and early 2000s A rising movement for independence began to emerge in Ukraine. In 1991, the proclamation of independence 1991 resulted from protests in the streets and political mobilisation.

National Building Challenges: During the post-Soviet period, Ukraine had to deal various problems, such as economic instability as well as political instability and corruption, as well as the challenging restoration of democratic institutions.

It was the Orange Revolution And The Yanukovych Presidency The year 2004 saw an uprising of the masses against corruption and election rigging in Ukraine. Viktor Yushchenko, a pro-Western presidential candidate, took the presidency in the event that it was changed because of the uprising.

Viktor Yanukovych: After winning the presidency election in 2010, the pro-Russian political figure Viktor Yanukovych raised worries among Ukrainians who wanted to build stronger relations to Europe. European Union.

Protests dubbed the Euromaidan demonstrations erupted at Kyiv's Maidan Nezalezhnosti (Independence Square) between late 2013 and the beginning of 2014, in protest against the decision to annex Crimea. The decision of the government to delay the signing of an association arrangement in conjunction with the European Union first set off the protests. In the wake of Euromaidan demonstrations Russia was able to take over Crimea during March 2014, asserting it was protecting rights of Russian natives and also demonstrating its strength in the area.

Conflict As Well As Pro-Russian Separation In Eastern Ukraine: Pro-Russian separatist movement first arose in the eastern region of Ukraine due to the incursion of Crimea as well as political changes within Kiev particularly within the Donetsk as well as Luhansk regions.

Chapter 8: Events Leading To The Conflict

Political Unrest and Power Shifts From 2004 To 2010

The allegations of widespread fraud during the presidential election in 2004 resulted in an Orange Revolution. Viktor Yushchenko won the rerun when the results of the elections were annulled because of protests and rallies. In the event that pro-Russian politician Viktor Yanukovych won the presidency in 2010, it signified that a shift in policies towards Russia. Yanukovych's Ukrainian government stated it was not going to negotiate an association deal with the EU to forge more ties with Russia. People were furious over the decision. Ukraine's pro-European citizens protested against the ruling party's decision to create Maidan Nezalezhnosti (Independence Square) in Kyiv in Kyiv, urging democracy, a halt corruption and closer ties to Europe.

The conflict between protesters and security officers resulted in an increase of the demonstrations. Many people were killed in the violence of the government's attempts to end protests. The violence only increased public resentment. Yanukovych's demise and the transition of power. The violent clashes between protesters and security officers signaled the turning stage during the Euromaidan protests. Following the murder of several protesters, Yanukovych fled the country and sought refuge to Russia. After the demise of Yanukovych, Ukraine created an interim government under the leadership of Premier Arseniy Yatsenyuk as well as Acting Presidency Oleksandr Turchynov. Russia provided soldiers into the autonomous republic in Crimea in Ukraine in February of 2014. Russia's pro-Russian militias joined forces with the Ukrainian army as they took over of key government structures as well as infrastructure.

The referendum on Crimea was a contentious one in Crimea during March of 2014 that Ukraine as well as a significant section of the world opposed. The result of the vote was the official annexation by Russia of Crimea.

Eastern Ukraine's Practice Of Pro-Russian Secession

Popularity of Russian-influenced views increased in the aftermath of the Russian taking over of Crimea and especially the cities of Donetsk as well as Luhansk. The cries were for greater autonomy and more links to Russia. The regions of Donetsk and Luhansk the self-declared "people's republics" were established by separatist leaders, who declared their independence from Ukraine and the desire for closer ties with Russia. The conflict is getting worse and so is the Russo-Ukrainian War. Combat erupted between pro-Russian separatists as well as Ukrainian state forces, as rebel activities of Donetsk and Luhansk were intensified. The military's operations, the shelling and fighting were fought during the conflict in a variety of Eastern Ukrainian cities and towns. Russia is accused of Ukraine as well as Western countries of providing support for the military, such as the provision of personnel, equipment and equipment to militant forces. While Russia did not deny direct engagement the evidence suggested a significant Russian military assistance. Public uprisings, political changes along with geopolitical maneuverings and then the annexation later of Crimea are all a part of the circumstances that triggered the Russo-Ukrainian War, which further inflamed separatist feelings and led to conflict in eastern Ukraine.

Ukrainian Revolution And Crimea's Annexation

The Euromaidan Revolution in Ukraine, often referred to as "the" Ukrainian Revolution, and Russia's later annexation of Crimea had a major role in the setting of the Russo-Ukrainian War.

Background

In November of 2013 The Ukrainian government had decided to postpone signing an agreement of association in the European Union (EU), which triggered the Ukrainian Revolution. The agreement is designed to enhance Ukrainian ties with the EU both on the front of economics and politics. Unrest in the public is the result of the decision to revoke the EU accord of association because the majority of Ukrainians believed that closer ties to Europe as vital to the process of the development of democracy, growth in economics, as well as separating their country from the influence of Russia. It was the Maidan Nezalezhnosti

(Independence Square) located in Kyiv became the central point of the Euromaidan demonstrations. They demanded for the resignation of President Viktor Yanukovych and the end of corruption, reforms to democracy as well as stronger ties to the EU. Protesters and security officers were a common sight as the demonstrations increased. An enervating crackdown on protestors during February 2014 caused violence to escalate and ended in the deaths of many individuals. The Ukrainian president Yanukovych was exiled from his country in February 2014 due to of the disorder and anger getting to a boiling point. Following that was over, the Ukrainian Parlament voted to oust Yanukovych. After Yanukovych's deposing, Russia profited from the turmoil within Ukrainian the political scene. The end of February 2014 saw without marking Russian military forces retreated into Crimea and seized crucial infrastructure and strategically important places.

Crimea held a referendum to make a decision on its status in the month of March of 2014. Because the vote was held before Russian forces, and without the permission of the Ukrainian administration, it came under severe criticism as being unjustified. Most voters, in the end agreed with the joining of Russia. Russia has officially annexed Crimea in the wake of the disputed vote results. The government claimed that the reason for this was in order to protect the rights of people of the ethnic Russian and the Russian-speaking people living of the area. This annexation was firmly condemned by the international community for being violation of Ukraine's sovereignty as well as the international legal system. In the aftermath of Russia gained the right to annexe Crimea relations between them were strained, which led to an increase in the conflict in the eastern part of Ukraine. Important key events, such as those of the Ukrainian Revolution and the acquisition of Crimea made the way for the Russo-Ukrainian War. The accession of Crimea intensified the conflict between the pro-Russian and pro-Ukrainian groups and spurred separatist movements within the eastern part of Ukraine But the Revolution exposed the aspirations of a large portion of Ukrainians to establish deeper connections to Europe as well as democratic change.

Euromaidan Protest

Euromaidan Also known by The Maidan Uprising, was a unrest and protests within Ukraine which started on November 21st, 2013 and culminated in large rallies at Ukraine's Maidan Nezalezhnosti (Independence Square). The unannounced decision of the president Viktor Yanukovych to reject the EU-Ukraine Association Agreement to promote more enlightened relations with Russia as well as the Eurasian Economic Union set off the protests. Even though this EU-Ukraine Agreement had been unanimously accepted by the Ukrainian legislature, Russia had pushed Ukraine to oppose the agreement. As Yanukovych was pushed to resign and for the Azarov government's removal, the scope of protests increased. The protesters criticized what they believed as widespread corruption in the government in power, abuse of power, violations of human rights and the oligarch's influence. Yanukovych was classified as a result of Transparency International as the foremost corrupt president around the globe. Further anger was sparked due to the brutal expulsion of protesters on the 30th of November. This year's Revolution for Dignity was sparked by Euromaidan.

Following the Euromaidan Uprising, and

Revolution for Dignity the following was the next:

The President is being removed from office Viktor Yanukovych from office

The ties to Russia ended.

Following the Russian military intervention and the Russian control of Crimea the protests to demand "United Ukraine" began on the 20th of February.

The Constitution of 2004 was once more being implemented.

Oleksandr Turchynov was named the acting president. Oleksandr Turchynov was made acting president.

Preliminary presidential elections.

The laws restricting civil liberties are adopted and then abrogated

Yulia Tymoshenko was the former leader of the government of Ukraine and prominent opposition leader she was freed from prison.

The role of local governments.

Local government bodies controlled by extremists opposed to government have banned from the Party of Regions.

Mykola Azarov, Ukraine's premier minister, steps down (President Yanukovych gives the opposition the position)

Independence Square (Maidan) in Kiev was a huge protest camp that took place during the uprising that was populated by hundreds of protesters and surrounded by handmade barrier.

The shocking announcement made by the Ukrainian government delay in signing an association agreement with EU caused protests. The agreement is designed to enhance Ukrainian ties with the EU in both the fronts of economic and political.

The majority of people who are pro-European think that a large part of Ukrainians considered the agreement as a significant step towards European integration that they believed would lead to opportunities for economic growth, changes in the democratic system as well as remove Ukraine from Russia's zone of influence. The decision to end the agreement was seen by the protesters as a step of the Ukrainian government to be closer to Russia and raises concerns about the deterioration of democratic principles as well as corruption and limitations on freedoms of the individual.

European Integration: The protesters stressed the necessity of more integration into European institutions and principles by insisting on the government to reverse its decision to join the European Union's Association Agreement.

Protests for political reforms revealed the general discontent with nepotism, corruption as well as the absence of transparency in Ukrainian political life. The demands included changes in the structure to combat corruption and promote an environment of transparency, along with the demise of the president Viktor Yanukovych and his team.

Human Rights And Freedoms: The protesters placed an intense importance on protecting the right of peaceful assembly, free speech and freedom of speech. The protesters sought to build an environment that is more democratic and inclusive.

The Mass Participation Movement: broad spectrum of socioeconomic and local communities comprising students, professionals, members of the civil public, and opposition politicians attracted to the demonstrations.

Occupation of Maidan Nezalezhnosti: Independence Square in Kyiv was used as the focal stage of protests in which protesters set up a camp, set up barricades and were there for a couple of months.

Civil Disobedience and Nonviolent Protests focussed on peaceful protests which included participants in non-violent protests or rallies, activities for culture and even civil protests.

The tensions between the government and the demonstrators grew violent as demonstrations went into the night. Protesters and security guards often clashed. This resulted in injuries and death.

Deathly Repression: By using the snipers and riot police as well as snipers, the Ukrainian government used violence to disperse the protesters in February of 2014. Many security guards and demonstrators were killed during the clashes as well as a number of others wounded.

Ousting Yanukovych: The brutal repression that followed and the deaths was a pivotal moment in the agitations.

President Yanukovych quit the country in addition, the Ukrainian Parliament finally removed Yanukovych from the presidency by disqualifying his predecessor. The Euromaidan demonstrations represented a significant moment in Ukrainian time, expressing what the citizens wanted seeking democratic reforms, greater openness as well as closer ties with Europe. However, the demonstrations have also opened the door to further social and political divides within Ukraine and laid the foundation for an eastern conflict Ukraine that ensued and later the annexed of Crimea.

Ousting Of President Viktor Yanukovych

The deposed president Viktor Yanukovych was a turning stage in Ukrainian political history and was a crucial occasion during the Euromaidan protests.

The Ukrainian government led by Yanukovych was under tension from protesters as well as opposition groups and even outsiders as the Euromaidan protests gained momentum in response to protesters demand for reforms in the political system and closer ties to Europe. As the conflict between security forces and protesters increased and numerous victims died, the protests were at a crossroads. Violence heightened the intensity of anger and calls for Yanukovych to quit. Yanukovych's popularity in the political arena decreased significantly when the situation deteriorated. Significant supporters and senior officials of his political party started to disengage from him. Negotiations and failed compromises Discussions between the government, opposition officials, and mediators from abroad were carried out to help diffuse the tension. The efforts, however, to create the consensus needed, for example an agreement to share power was not successful. Yanukovych abruptly quit Kyiv and headed for Russia for peace on February 21 2014. Yanukovych's departure has left Ukraine in a state of powerlessness and an impression of political insecurity. It was the Ukrainian parliament (Verkhovna Rada) swiftly moved to remove Yanukovych following his defection. The Ukrainian constitution was violated According to the Parliament as well as Yanukovych was not performing his duties. When Yanukovych was removed from his post, Ukraine created an interim administration, headed by the Prime Minister Arseniy Yatsenyuk as well as Acting Presidency Oleksandr Turchynov. To settle the crisis and get ready to hold fresh elections, Ukraine created an temporary administration.

Former President Viktor Yanukovych and Vladimir Putin

After Yanukovych's ouster the country, many Western nations, particularly that of the United States and other European nations, endorsed the new Ukrainian government. Russia condemned the actions that took place in Ukraine and viewed Yanukovych's ouster as a coup that was not constitutional and backed by the West. Russian officials expressed concern about security and rights of the ethnic Russians as well as Russian natives within Ukraine but also refused to recognise the current Ukrainian government.

A Ukrainian justice court sentenced Yanukovych in absentia to 13 years of prison for treason in high-level felony on the 24th of January, 2019. In the years since his resignation, Yanukovych has received the lowest social poll ratings and is ranked as the most unpopular president in Ukrainian time. Yanukisms which is the term that is used by Yanukovych for a description of blunders committed by Ukrainian political leaders, is the name of his predecessor. His removal from power was a significant change in Ukrainian political life, bringing an era of turmoil and unpredictable. This also opened the door to escalate tensions among Russia and Ukraine that eventually resulted in an outbreak of the Russo-Ukrainian War and the annexation of Crimea.

Intensification and Expansion Of HostilitiesRussian forces were in Crimea towards the end of February 2014. They did not have official identification, but they generally believed to have been Russian soldiers. Critical infrastructure, governmental structures, as well as military installations were quickly taken over by the control of their. A referendum was that was held in Crimea in the month of March 2014 large majority of voters favored taking part in Russia. Ukraine as well as a significant part of the world condemned the vote as not being valid. Russia officially added Crimea following the referendum, saying it was doing it to safeguard the rights of people of the ethnic Russian and the Russian-speaking population. Some people opposed the decision as a violation of international law and Ukrainian sovereignty. The pro-Russian separatists who were sometimes aided with Russian military and soldiers were able to take control of the public facilities across a variety of east Ukrainian cities and towns, creating the so-called "people's republics." Security efforts were launched in the name of Ukrainian government in order to restore authority over the territories it had taken control of and to put a stop to militant groups. To halt the separatist attacks and to restore order in regions affected, the government forces were deployed. The conflict between the government troops and rebels from Russia grew while the Ukrainian government attempted to regain the control. Both sides had casualties and infrastructure was damaged severely. Russia is accused by Ukraine as well as a number of Western nations of supplying troops, equipment and various other types of assistance for military to rebel forces. Even though the Russian government denies the involvement of its own troops, there is evidence towards a significant military assistance provided by Russia. The eastern conflict Ukraine has been increasingly considered an indirect conflict in the region between Ukraine and Russia and Russia, with Russia being said to be helping rebels in advancing its geopolitical goals and strategic objectives as Ukraine tried to preserve its territorial sovereignty. In addition to Donetsk and Luhansk the additional eastern Ukrainian areas like Kharkiv and Dnipropetrovsk were witness to the development of separatist movements as well as conflicts with authorities. Major losses of life as well as the destruction of infrastructure and thousands of displaced persons caused a human catastrophe in the aftermath of conflict. Both sides were convicted of infringing on international humanitarian law as well as the human rights of others.

The annexed territory of Crimea and the rise of pro-Russian separatist movements in the eastern part of Ukraine as well as the subsequent combats and military operations between separatist groups as well as Ukrainian military personnel all led to an increase in violence and the commencement of hostilities within the Russo-Ukrainian conflict. The political climate within Ukraine as well as the security of the area around as well as international relations remain significantly affected from the war. The popularity of pro-Russian views increased within the eastern Ukrainian regions following Russia gained the annexation of Crimea particularly within Donetsk as well as Luhansk. Separatist groups that seek more autonomy and ties to Russia started to appear. In the eastern Ukrainian cities, such as Donetsk and Luhansk the pro-Russian militants removed government offices, the police stations and other critical infrastructure. Separatist leaders declared "people's republics" in Donetsk and Luhansk in which they declared the independence of these cities from Ukraine and vowing to make their country more like Russia. The military operations were initiated through the Ukrainian government in order to restore authority over the areas it had taken and end the separatist activities. They attempted to bring an end to rebels' uprisings, preserve the integrity of Ukraine's territory in order to restore the law and law and. Conflicts that were violent between Ukrainian authorities as well as separatist organisations resulted from military actions. Both sides used heavy weapons like rifles, artillery and various other heavy weapons that caused significant damage as well as deaths in the affected zones.

The humanitarian disaster was the result of the conflict due to internally displaced of thousands of individuals, destruction to the infrastructure, as well as disruptions to crucial services.

Russia is blamed by Ukraine as well as Western nations of offering the rebels in Ukraine a lot of help in the form of weapons, supplies and personnel from the military. While Russia has denied any direct involvement there is evidence of substantial Russian military aid. According to the reports, Russian troops crossed the line across Ukraine and engaged in battle against rebel organizations. The international media have been expressing concern and tension due to the Russian military's participation in Ukraine.

Everyone onboard Malaysia Airlines Flight MH17 were killed in the incident that took place when it was shot down in eastern Ukraine in July of 2014. This incident raised the bar of global review and criticism of the ongoing conflict. Western nations, notably those of the United States and the European Union were able to sanction Russia economically to protest the situation's escalated. The talks were conducted through channels similar to the Minsk agreement in an effort to come to a peaceable conclusion by diplomatic means. It was not easy despite a number of cease-fires and peace agreements which was accompanied by constant fighting, shelling and deaths in the eastern part of Ukraine.

Chapter 9: Pro-Russian Separatism In Eastern Ukraine

When the United Nations General Assembly voted for the territorial integrity of Ukraine during the initial phase of the conflict between February and March 2014. Russia was able to strike and eventually captured Crimea, which is in the Ukrainian area of Crimea. As a parallel event, anti-Maidan as well as pro-Russian rallies were staged across several regions in northern and eastern Ukraine. The beginning of March 2014 was when local separatists seized advantage of the current situation to take control of the government structures within the oblasts of Donetsk, Luhansk, and Kharkiv. A portion of the rebels were backed and financed by Russian security services. The uprising was quickly ended by Ukrainian authorities who declared rebels gone before the 10th of March. Armed groups with the support of Russia took over government buildings within areas of the Donetsk and Luhansk Oblasts, also known as the Donbas in the second period that started in April 2014. This triggered an insurgency by separatists that erupted there. The Ukrainian government launched what described as an "Anti-Terrorist Operation" (ATO) which involved the army to stop the uprising.Despite the death of many of demonstrators mostly from Russia and the escalating violence within Odessa and Kharkiv oblasts Kharkiv and Odessa regions did not escalate into a major conflict. Thanks to the local authority for civil affairs the order was restored the areas of Odessa and Kharkiv, however the pro-Russian protests such as bombings continued throughout the entire throughout the. Russians who were on the opposite part of the border that were there to help pro-Russian militants in Ukraine were part of the Pro-Russian protesters. Serhiy Taruta who is the

Governor of Donetsk oblast, said that Donetsk region, stated that residents who came from Crimea as well as ex-convicts took part in protests held in Donetsk. Between March 4 and 25 the Ukrainian border guards and the police refused to admit over 8200 Russians. In the words of Andriy Parubiy who is the secretary of the National Security and Defense Council between 500 and 700 Russians were denied entry each daily. Russia has claimed it was they were able to use United States used proxies to influence the popular uprising that took place in Ukraine during 2014. To help make Ukraine more attractive at the eyes of investors Yanukovych is against IMF mandated economic reforms. Russian government officials have claimed that they believed that the American National Endowment for Democracy has sparked anti-Yanukovych opposition. After the refusal of the changes, the Oleksandr Tychnov-led interim government pushed through the reforms after receiving a $13 billion credit from the IMF as well as additional funding from USAID.

The Ukrainians' support for unification with Russia was studied from February 8-18, 2014 by Kyiv's International Institute for Sociology (KIIS). In the end, it was found that 12percent of the people polled supported unification with Russia. 68.0 percent of those surveyed believed Ukraine should keep its autonomy as well as its cordial relations with Russia.

In a number of oblasts, it was evident that the the support for unions among Russia with Ukraine was much higher than the following:

41.0% Crimea

33.2% Donetsk Oblast

24.1% Luhansk Oblast

24.0% Odessa Oblast

16.7% Zaporizhia Oblast

15.1% Kharkiv Oblast

13.8% Dnipropetrovsk Oblast

A follow-up poll by Kyiv's International Institute of Socialology in April across all eastern and southern Ukrainian Oblasts, with the exception of Crimea (which was added to Russia in the time of this poll) and found that the overwhelming majority of respondents were against the secession of Ukraine as well as annexation by Russia across all oblasts, except for those in the Donbas (Donetsk as well as Luhansk Oblasts).

The percentage of those that chose "Rather, no" and "Certainly, no, I don't" in response to the question of whether they were opposed to an independent Ukraine Ukraine as well as Russian annexed territories was the following in different regions of eastern and southern Ukrainian Oblasts:

51.9% Luhansk Oblast

52.2% Donetsk Oblast

65.6% Kharkiv Oblast

78.8% Odessa Oblast

81.5% Zaporizhia Oblast

84.1% Dnipropetrovsk Oblast

84.6% Kherson Oblast

85.4% Mykolaiv Oblast

A survey conducted by the International Republican Institute between March 14 to March 26, between 26-27% respondents from eastern and southern Ukraine thought they were seeing that the Euromaidan protests as the result of a coup. In the eastern part of Ukraine only

5percent of those surveyed claimed that they "definitely" felt threatened or in danger or under pressure. A mere 13% of the respondents from southern Ukraine and 22% of those in the eastern part of Ukraine considered that the Russian actions in Crimea were in defense of Ukrainians who were fluent in Russian and 37 percent and 30 percent believed that they represented an attack and occupation. A second survey from KIIS which was conducted between 8-16 April discovered that a significant majority of those surveyed were against the police's repression of public buildings. In the eastern and southern regions of Ukraine over half of those surveyed believed that Oleksandr Turchynov, who was the interim president, was unlegitimate. Most of those who responded in eastern and southern Ukraine said that maintaining the nation's unity requires the de-arming and the dissolution of illegal extreme groups. 19.1

percent of respondents from eastern and southern Ukraine considered that Ukraine ought to be an autonomous state. 45.2 percent thought Ukraine ought to be an autonomous state with decentralized powers to regional regions. The majority of respondents believed the idea that Russia as well as Ukraine should have open border without the need for visas as well as 8.4 percent believed that Ukraine and Russia could be joined to create an independent state. The idea of a federation for Ukraine was backed by 24.8 percent of those surveyed as was the decision to secession regions to become part of with the Russian Federation by 15.4% of those surveyed. A majority of those who were surveyed said that they were not able to think Russia appealing however those who chose to do so did it primarily for commercial instead of cultural motives. In the end, it was clear that the credibility of present government and the parliament was mostly contestable among people who were that were interviewed in eastern and southern Ukraine however, most people across all regions were of the opinion that Viktor Yanukovych wasn't the rightful head of the nation. Petro Poroshenko who is a pro-Euromaidan theoligarch, was in charge of elections in the early stages of all regions, with the exception of Donbas. It was the Pew Research Centre conducted a comprehensive study of the opinions within Ukraine regarding the conflict, which was released on the 8th of May. The survey was carried out following the weaning of Crimea however, it was conducted prior to the clashes on May 2, in Odessa. 73% of the respondents from the eastern region and 93% of those from the west said they would like Ukraine to remain unified.Despite widespread opposition across all over the world, the Crimea referendum which took place on the 16th of March in the region, 91% of those polled in the region thought the vote was fair and fair. In addition, 88% believed that the Ukrainian government should be able to accept the result. There were rumors throughout the Euromaidan movement that Yanukovych as well as Russian supporters as well as anti-Maidan protesters were receiving money to assist. Political expert Oleksiy Haran, from the Kyiv Mohyla Academy said that "those in the anti-Maidan movement are a source of cash only. They are hired guns employed by the authorities to create the opposition. They aren't taking any risks. Oleg Bakhtiyarov, the chief of the extreme Eurasian Youth Union in Russia was arrested because he urged protesters to assist in the destruction of government buildings in exchange for $500 each. In the Internal Affairs Ministry reported on April 13 that a group of recruiters were found to have paid 500 to take part in the riots and 40 dollars to take over facilities.

Party of Regions member Volodymyr Landik as well as First Vice-Prime Minister Vitaliy Yarema, author Serhiy Leshchenko, as well as an analysis released from the Organization for Security and Co-operation in Europe each of which is backed by accounts of protesters paid.

Declaration Of Independence In Donetsk And Luhansk

The Ukrainian Donbas area, there are two Russian civil-military government systems, called the Donetsk People's Republic (DPR) as well as the Luhansk People's Republic (LPR). While they are only in possession of a fraction of the territories they claim in November 2022 Russia declares it has acquired them as an integral part of its territory and considers them as federal sovereign subjects. They declared independence from Ukraine in the month of October however, the world continues to view the region as a component of Ukraine's own sovereign territories. Rebels declared the DPR as well as the LPR in the course of the 2014 Donbass War with Russian help. The militants who control the two republics conducted independence referendums on May 11th in 2014. Except for Russia however, none of the nations recognized the results of the referendum. The Ukrainian government was adamant about recognizing the separatists pro-Russian as terrorists. It was the "Novorossiya" union that the DPR and LPR tried to establish in 2014 ended up being disbanded at the end of 2015. South Ossetia, a separate state within Georgia recognized the autonomy of the two regions in 2014.

On the 21st of February, 2022 Russia declared them sovereign republics.

Abkhazia is a separate autonomous region within Georgia has been recognized just four days after. Two other UN members have since acknowledged the DPR as well as the LPR: Syria on June 29th, 2022 as well as North Korea on July 13 2022.

In September 30th 2022 Russia officially annexed both the DPR as well as the LPR.

Role Of Russia In The Conflict

Russia held a tense referendum in Crimea which resulted in the vote of joining Russia but it was not accepted by Ukraine as well as the international world. Following that, Russia formally added Crimea to its territories.

Following the time that Crimea was annexed by Russia, pro-Russian separatist groups were able to grow in the Eastern Ukrainian areas, particularly Donetsk as well as Luhansk. These movements sought greater autonomy or independence from Ukraine and close ties with Russia.

Russia is accused of offering the separatists a significant support. This includes supplies with weapons, as well as military personnel. Tanks, artillery as well as surface-to-air missile systems are all part of this support. There is evidence to suggest that Russian military forces were directly involved in the battle. There are reports of Russian troops entering Ukraine in order to help rebels.

It has also included the involvement of Russian special troops, regular soldiers and even spies. The separatists have profited significantly from the crucial support provided by Russia's Russian military has provided the separatists, such as instruction, commands and control, logistical support and sharing of information. The tenacity and effectiveness of the separatist movement has benefited greatly from this. The east Ukraine areas ruled by separatists have been given help from Russia. This is in the form of financial aid as well as infrastructure initiatives designed to improve the control of these regions and to promote connections to Russia at a commercial scale.

In announcing the self-declared "people's republics" in Donetsk and Luhansk as well as advancing their standing in the international arena, Russia has also politically assisted separatists. Russia has been a part of talks and discussions to bring an end to this conflict. Participating in talks through different avenues, like the Minsk agreements, fall into this class. In the wake of allegations of continuing Russian support for rebels, and violations of ceasefire, nevertheless, implementing ceasefire agreements and the conclusion of the war are challenging. Russian support for separatists was important, however it was secret as well as attempts from authorities of Ukrainian government to completely recover the territory held by separatists failed. Russian forces were involved in the conflict in spite of the fact that Russia denies involvement. In the Minsk II accords to stop the conflict were signed by Russia as well as Ukraine in February 2015 however, they weren't fully adopted in the years following. A few temporary ceasefires were in place, but not a lasting peace, as well as a limited shift in territory, the Donbas conflict among Ukraine and Russian proxies turned out to be violent conflict that was not able to be resolved with only a few minor changes to territory control.

In 2021 the first phase of this was when Russia has increased its presence in the military along its frontier with Ukraine as well as in Belarus which is a neighbouring country. The plans to take over Ukraine have been repeatedly rejected by Russian official. Vladimir Putin, the president of Russia has criticized the expansion of NATO and demanded for Ukraine be prevented from becoming a member of the alliance. In addition, he voiced his irredentist beliefs and doubted Ukraine's legitimate in its existence.

The role in the involvement of Russia in the conflict between Ukraine and Russia is causing alarm and condemnation across the globe. Financial penalties, increased tensions among Russia and Western countries, and the deterioration of diplomatic relations have all caused by Russian actions. Stability, integrity as well as the geopolitical environment in Ukraine remain profoundly affected by the current conflict.

Chapter 10: Accusations And Denials Of Russian Involvement

And Allegations

Support from the military The separatists of the eastern region of Ukraine appear to be receiving military assistance directly from Russia according to Ukraine as well as Western countries. The separatists are given access to weapons, ammunition and other military-related equipment.

troop deployments Reports have surfaced of Russian troops coming into Ukraine across the border, as well as fighting the rebels. The claims are supported with evidence such as captured soldiers as well as weapons with Russian emblems.

Command and Control Command and Control: It's been said that Russia is in charge of the separatist forces providing them with assistance in military coordination, as well as strategic guidance.

The supply channels: According sources, Russia has set up supply channels that include convoys that carry troops and supplies to those in the regions controlled by separatists.

Refutations And Rebuttals.

Official denials A: Russian government has repeatedly denied that it has a hand in the war, insisting that the Russians engaged in Ukraine do so on their own initiative and do not follow instructions from their governments. Russia recognizes that nation's citizens are fighting Ukraine however, it insists that they are self-governing members driven by their own beliefs. Russia is denying claims that separatists are equipped with Russian equipment, saying that the weapons could be from different sources, or taken from prisoners by Ukrainian security forces.

False Flags and Provocations: Based on the information provided by Russian officials, Ukraine has staged provocations as well as false flag activities to make it appear as if there is Russian engagement and to gain the backing from countries around the world.

International Perspectives

Numerous independent investigations, such as ones conducted by international organisations and news media and media outlets, have provided evidence to support claims that there was Russian involvement. The evidence includes satellite images as well as intercepted messages, as well as witness testimony. Western nations, such as those of the United States and European nations are consistently supporting the claims of Russian involvement in the conflict and have put sanctions against Russia to counter. Negotiations to settle conflicts, like Minsk ag Minsk accusations of Russian involvement, have been confirmed by several independent investigations, such as the ones carried out by international organizations and media publications. The evidence is based on witnesses' testimony, conversations intercepted as well as satellite imagery. In the United States and other Western countries, particularly those of Europe are repeatedly supporting claims of Russian involvement and have punished Russia with sanctions on its economy due to. The Minsk agreement, which was a part of the diplomatic attempt to resolve the conflict included provisions that addressed the issue of Russian involvement as well as the expulsion of foreign troops and military equipment out of Ukrainian territories. There are a variety of contradictory accounts and discussions revolve around the issue of Russian participation in the Russian-Ukrainian war that continues to cause a lot of controversy. Even though Ukraine as well as many Western nations believe Russia has been actively involved in the war, Russia continues to deny any direct military involvement and claims that its troops' participation to fight is independent and free.

Evidence Of Russian Support To Separatist Forces

The paramilitary separatist groups began to appear in 2014 amid the pro-Russian turmoil in Ukraine. When they were forming the Army of the South-East was established at Luhansk Oblast, Pavel Gubarev established his organization, the Donbas People's Militia and proclaimed himself to be the "People's Governor" of Donetsk Oblast in March of 2014. The Donbas conflict began in April 2014 in the aftermath of these groups taking over Ukrainian government buildings in the region. This prompted the Ukrainian military to launch the anti-terrorist operations. Through the course of war, Russian far-right organizations recruited massively for separatists and a few far-right activists joined as volunteer groups. The paramilitaries belonging to the separatists were accused of war crimes including the shooting down of the Malaysia Airlines flight and the attacks by rockets on Mariupol and Mariupol, both of which they deny. They are also responsible for the illegal kidnapping of detainees, torture, and abduction of civilians throughout the Donbas region.

The separatist paramilitaries were supported by and served as proxy of Russia. Russian Armed Forces. Although Russia has denied its involvement directly, the evidence indicated otherwise. The separatists admitted receiving weapons as well as supplies from Russia and were undergoing training in Russia as well as being able to count Russian members in their members. In September of 2015, Russian Army officers were leading separatist troops at the battalion-level and above. The year 2023 was the first time Russia recognized separatists' fighters as Russian veteran combatants. As the year progressed for the Russian attack, the states of the separatists made conscription mandatory and forced men to combat to defend Russia. The soldiers of in the Donbas region were considered "cannon fodder" for the Russian forces, which resulted in a high rate of casualties. According to official sources, separatists had the possibility of a nearly 50% casualty number among separatist forces until the month of November 2022. There are numerous evidences to back the assertions of Russian assistance to rebel forces. These include satellite images monitoring the movements of Russian military equipment, as well as the arrest of military personnel and other equipment bearing Russian designs, intercepted messages between Russian military personnel, testimony from former witnesses and fighters, independent investigations confessions made by Russian volunteers and soldiers, as well as using open-source intelligence and social media for gathering data. These evidences as well as other evidence are given by Ukrainian officials along with international investigators as well as Western nations to confirm the claim that there was Russian support for the rebels in Eastern Ukraine. Although Russia has repeatedly denied this, Russia The evidence suggests a substantial amount of Russian assistance, which includes providing arms, equipment, and personnel as well as strategic direction.

The Impact Of Russian Involvement On The Conflict

The separatists now enjoy a massive advantage on the battlefield due to Russian aid. They have improved their skills through the use of state-of-the-art weapons, equipment as well as ammunition. This has allowed them to effectively fight Ukrainian military activities.

Russia's involvement Russia is also helping the rebel forces to become better trained and organized, improving the effectiveness of their fight and coordination.

Russian military aid is a major factor in the conflict's increase in intensity. Separatist groups are successful in restraining the Ukrainian government, and continue to rule large areas of east Ukraine. Russian assistance, such as the supply of equipment as well as reinforcements, has helped the separatists to stand up to Ukrainian military incursions and keep their areas of control. The presence of Russian army personnel and their equipment has resulted in an increase in violence within the war. Heavy weaponry including tanks, artillery and other weapons results in more deaths as well as significant destruction to civilian and infrastructure. This conflict has led to numerous civilian deaths, injuries and displacements, as in the form of military deaths from both sides. Eastern Ukraine has become more unstable because of Russian intervention and has had significant economic, social and political implications. The infrastructure, the government, as well as the situation for humanitarian aid are all impacted due to conflict and the annexation of territory by separatist organizations. In addition, the presence of regimes that are separatist which are supported by Russia has placed the Ukrainian authorities in danger and has slowed initiatives to get the region back to peace and security. Russian participation in this war has had wider geopolitical implications. The conflict has caused tension between Russia as well as Western nations, which has led to diplomatic tensions, sanctions on the economy as well as a general decline of relationships between the two countries. This conflict also has raised fears about Russia's intentions as well as activities in the post-Soviet sphere which has resulted in a reconsideration of the security situation within the region. The peace process as well as diplomacy efforts to resolve the war have been hampered due to Russian involvement. There are separatist groups that are backed by Russia as well as ongoing military aid has made negotiations and implementation of ceasefire agreements harder. To achieve a long-lasting peace, Russia needs to be involved active participation in peace process because of its influence over separatists and its strategic interests in the region.

The involvement of Russia during the Russo-Ukrainian War had a significant impact, altering the character of the conflict, increasing the human suffering, as well as changing the geopolitical landscape in the region. A resolution to the war and the reconstruction of peace in Ukraine is contingent on solving the issues that are posed by Russian involvement, and identifying the diplomatic means to address fundamental issues that fuel the war.

Humanitarian And Security Implications

It was 2022. Russian attack on Ukraine was a major human-rights consequences that impacted both Ukraine and the world community. The consequences of this include the rise from the Ukrainian refugee crisis, interruptions in global food supply, massive conscription across Russia as well as Ukraine as well as severe consequences to Ukrainian society. The crisis of refugees that started in the latter part of February 2022 Europe was an immediate result of the Russian invasion of Ukraine. As of today, more than 8.2 million people fleeing Ukraine are documented throughout Europe in the past, while around 8 million were internally displaced within the country since late May 2022. In March, around quarter of the Ukrainian inhabitants had been forced to move out of their residences. It's worth noting that around 90percent of Ukrainian refugees are children and women however, the majority of Ukrainian men between the ages of 18 and 60 are not allowed to leave the nation. In March on, over half of the children living in Ukraine had been forced to leave, while a quarter having left the country. The refugee crisis that resulted of the war is the biggest one in Europe ever since World War II, the first in Europe after during the Yugoslav Wars in the 1990s as well as the fourth-largest ever refugee crisis. The crisis is also the most significant refugees' crisis in the 21st century with the largest rate of refugee movement across the globe.

Most refugees looked for refuge in countries west of Ukraine which included Poland, Slovakia, Hungary, Romania, and Moldova. In the following years, about 3 million refugees travelled further to the west of European countries. As per UNHCR information on October 18, 2022, countries that were receiving the most quantity of Ukrainian refugees included Russia (2.77 millions), Poland (1.5 million), Germany (1 million) and The Czech Republic (0.5 million). Human Rights Watch documented in September 2022 that Ukrainian civilians were forced to be relocated to Russia. Human Rights Watch has confirmed that the UN Human Rights Office has admitted credible claims of forced transfer of children who are not accompanied in Russian-occupied areas or the Russian Federation in its own territory. It is estimated by the United States Department of State estimates that close to 900,000 Ukrainian citizens were forcefully transferred to Russia. But, as of the time of the conflict over 4.5 million Ukrainians returned home to their country of origin. European Union (EU) countries which have borders with Ukraine are granting entry to everyone Ukrainian refugee refugees. In addition, the EU has enacted to invoke the Temporary Protection Directive, which permits Ukrainians to work, stay as well as study within any EU member country for a period of one year. It is crucial to remember that a few non-European and Romani persons have been reported to experience an influx of discrimination based on ethnicity at the border.

Agriculture And Food Supply Problem

The Ukrainian Defense Ministry charged that Russia has robbed "hundreds of thousands of tonnes of grain" from grain elevators and storage facilities across the entire Ukraine. Ukraine and was able to transport the grain to markets for sale. Large amounts of farm equipment such as combine harvesters, tractor, as well as other types of vehicles are also being taken from dealerships and farms and shipped to Russia In some cases, from as far as Chechnya. In the case of Ukraine's seize, theft of grains from its territory has the potential of cause food crises to get worse as well as The Ukrainian Ministry of Agriculture as well as the United Nations World Food Programme have issued cautions about the thefts could cause worse for Ukraine's food shortage and could cause more hunger in the world. The 30th of May Russia stated that it began importing grains from Kherson and had also begun to get sunflower seeds.

"If Kiev resolves the issue of demining ports, the Russian Navy will ensure the unhindered passage of ships carrying grain to the Mediterranean Sea," said Sergey Lavrov, the minister of foreign affairs in Russia. The Russian military has been accused of plucking the strawberries of Kherson Oblast, according to people living there. Senegalese president Macky Sall, the chairman of the African Union, met with Russian President Vladimir Putin on June 3 to discuss the "liberation of the stocks of grain and fertilizers," According to the office of President Sall and also to look at methods "to contribute to the lull of the war in Ukraine." The president said the situation is worsening due to EU sanctions on Russian bank accounts and products.

As per the UK MoD The UK Ministry of Defence says that according to the UK MoD, Ukrainian yield of 2022's grain will yield 35% of the 2021 yield. 14 vessels carrying various cereals and corn had successfully left Ukrainian ports since the 12th of August. The two first ones have been covered by an agreement with the United Nations. As per Ukrainian president Volodymyr Zelenskyy, as at the 26th of August Ukraine had exported nearly one million tons of grains. Around 44 vessels traveled to 15 nations. There are 70 vessels needing to be loaded up with grains. The president in Ukraine his stated goal is to produce 3 million tonnes per month. But until 2023, that target has slowed down.

Chapter 11: International Response And Diplomatic Efforts

A worldwide outrage over criticism of Russian aggression in Ukraine caused the enactment of new sanctions on Russia and sparked another financial crisis within the country. States have usually reacting negatively, especially in Europe as well as the Americas and Southeast Asia. A number of powerful countries, such as countries like the United Kingdom, the United States, Canada, France, Germany, Italy, Japan as well as Spain are among those that have criticised and condemned the current situation. Volodymyr Zelenskyy is the President of Ukraine has demanded or a no-fly zone is put in place over Ukraine or receive air assistance. Zelenskyy has also issued an "peace" appeal, saying that he didn't "want Ukraine's history to be a legend about 300 Spartans." Zelenskyy also cited Winston Churchill in a speech before members of the British House of Commons, declaring, "We will fight at sea, we will fight in the air, and we will protect our land." We are not going to surrender and will combat everywhere.

Russian troops who were captured or killed were documented through images as well as videos released by Ukrainian officials. Videos of soldiers being detained are said to be prohibited by Article 13 of the Third Geneva Convention According to a few experts.

On the 2nd of April, Zelenskyy advised Ukrainian residents that Russian troops have been "mining the entire territory" while they retreated from the region surrounding Kiev. They have removed "a lot of trip wires and other dangers" as well as they are also mining "homes, mining equipment, even the bodies of people who were killed." To assist those afflicted by the crisis, a number of countries and international organisations are providing aid to the affected. Assistance for water, food shelter, medical treatments as well as sanitary assistance for people who have been displaced and the impacted communities are all covered in the assistance. Monitoring and confirming ceasefires as well as the implementation of the Minsk agreements have been crucial duties to the OSCE. To keep track of the conditions in the field, record violations and encourage dialogue between parties, an OSCE Special Monitoring Mission (SMM) is being dispatched. They are taking out "a lot of trip wires and other dangers" and they are also extracting "homes, mining equipment, even the bodies of people who were killed." In order to help those affected by the crisis, a number of governments and international organizations have provided humanitarian assistance. Help for food, water shelter, medical treatments as well as sanitary assistance for people who have been displaced and the impacted communities are all part of the aid. Monitoring and verifying the ceasefire and implementation of the Minsk agreements have been crucial missions of the OSCE. To monitor the situation in the field as well as document any violations and encourage communication between Parties and the OSCE, an OSCE Special Monitoring Mission (SMM) was dispatched.

NATO's Response And Military Build Up In Eastern Europe

Military and political solutions are being offered by NATO as a response to the ongoing conflict that has been brewing between Russia and Ukraine in the Ukraine conflict, with a particular focus on strengthening the capabilities of NATO as well as its presence within Eastern Europe.

Enhanced Forward Presence (eFP)

The Enhanced Forward Presence plan of NATO has been put in place in response to the evolving security situation across Eastern Europe. It involves the rotating the deployment of multilateral battle groups for Poland, Estonia, Latvia as well as Lithuania. As a response to Russian activities in Ukraine The eFP will demonstrate NATO's commitment to protection of their Eastern European partners, strengthen the deterrent, and provide faith.

NATO created its Readiness Action Plan (RAP) in 2014 in order to enhance the level of preparedness and respond when faced with threats to security, including the conflict in the Russian-Ukrainian region.

The strategy calls for action that include more training in addition to equipment prepositioning increased capability of the military. The aim of the RAP is ensure NATO forces are prepared to stand up against any attack against the alliance members.

Marine patrols and air policing are being stepped up by NATO in order to secure and secure the Baltic states' airspaces, being visible and stopping any violations. To ensure and ensure the safety of the territorial waters of NATO allies and maritime patrols, and around the Baltic as well as the Black Seas have also been enhanced.

Military exercises: to increase interoperability, readiness as well as deterrence, NATO has undertaken a several military exercises across Eastern Europe and the surrounding zone.

An interesting exercise one of the most notable is the Defender series that includes both NATO members and partners and is focused on large-scale defense as well as scenario-based deterrents.

Through various organizations, including the NATO-Ukraine Annual National Programme as well as the NATO Georgia Joint Training and Evaluation Centre, NATO has improved its collaboration with its partner countries in the region, specifically Ukraine as well as Georgia. The programs aim to improve the defense capabilities of partner countries and cooperation, as well as aid in ensuring stability and security throughout the region.

NATO has taken measures to enhance defence and deterrence throughout Eastern Europe, but the NATO alliance has also emphasized the importance of maintaining an open line of communication as well as interaction with Russia.

As well as maintaining a robust defense posture, NATO is expressing its desire to participate in constructive discussions and seek ways to calm the situation and look for ways to resolve conflicts.

The response of the alliance and its militarism throughout Eastern Europe demonstrate its dedication to collective defense, deterrence as well as the safety of the member states. With regard to the Russo-Ukrainian War, these actions will help strengthen NATO's position in the region and improve interoperability among member states as well as send a clear signal of unity and dedication to the security of the alliance's Eastern European partners.

Influence On European Security Architecture

The conflict has caused the loss of confidence between Russia as well as several Western nations, not just countries that are part of the European security system. Conventions of international law have been violated and the pillars of cooperative security are being eroded because of the annexation by Russia of Crimea as well as its backing of the separatists in the eastern part of Ukraine. The risk to European security has been reviewed with regard to the Russian-Ukrainian conflict. The conflict has highlighted the potential for an attack by armed force as well as the necessity of protecting the sovereignty of our nation and its territorial integrity. There are concerns about the likelihood that similar attacks could occur elsewhere in areas that have territorial disputes or separatist groups were raised during the conflict, resulting in new interest in resolving the issues that could lead to chaos. This crisis has forced European nations to reconsider their deterrent and military capabilities and capabilities, particularly those close to Russia. The national defense forces are strengthened, the military's readiness has increased, and NATO's defense has improved. The significance for NATO in its role as an international security partnership for the member countries was reaffirmed following its involvement in the Russo-Ukrainian War. The war has forced NATO to enhance its capability as well as its presence throughout Eastern Europe and to take steps to boost its ability and ability to respond. This war also demonstrated the importance of NATO countries to keep in close cooperation and stand together in the face of changing security threats. Certain consequences of this war has altered the nature of security in the region, particularly those in Eastern Europe.

The war has created conflict and hostilities among Russia as well as Western countries, which has led to an increasingly hostile relation. For the sake of improving their security and to defend their own against attack in the future certain Eastern European nations have been motivated by war to establish closer relations with NATO as well as with the European Union. The conflict has impacted the efforts of Europe to build confidence and controlling armaments. There have been questions raised regarding the validity of agreements in place like those in the Treaty on Conventional Armed Forces in Europe (CFE), and efforts to increase confidence and co-operation among Russia as well as Western nations are hindered because of the breach of Ukraine's sovereignty as well as territorial integrity. Its implications regarding Europe's energy security emerged due to the current conflict. This has prompted attention to the extent to which certain European nations are of Russian energy sources in addition to the potential for disruptions in energy supply or threats during times of political unrest. In the course of this war, Russo-Ukrainian War has had a major impact upon Europe's security architecture. European Security Architecture, causing the need to reevaluate security concerns and a greater emphasis on defences, as well as a change in the regional dynamic. The war has highlighted the importance collaboration, teamwork and collective security when it comes to tackling emerging challenges while ensuring the stability of Europe.

Current Status And Future Prospects

In 2023 it is 2023 and in 2023, the Russo-Ukrainian War is still raging. Russia is now focused on consolidating its power in the Donbas region, as the war is entering the next phase. Russian forces have sustained massive losses in the face of Ukrainian forces. Ukrainian army, and the war has come to an impasse. The outlook for the future remain uncertain. Russia might decide to start an attack from a different area of Ukraine or continue harassing Ukrainian soldiers within the Donbas. In addition, the war could last for a long time without either winner winning by an obvious difference. Ukraine has endured a number of devastating consequences of the conflict. Its economy is in a state of decline, and thousands of people are displaced. The war is having a major impact on the global economy too, resulting in rising prices for energy and disrupting supply lines. It's a world-wide issue with wide-ranging implications. It has intensified Western as well as Russian tensions as well as changed the way European security is perceived. It will be fascinating see how the international community responds in the coming years because the conflict acts as a testing of global stability.

Future Possibilities For The Russian-Ukrainian War Might Include:

An agreement on a settlement that is negotiated Two parties could come to an agreement which calls for an end in hostilities, as well as the evacuation of Russian troops. All parties agree that this is the most desirable outcome because it will put an end calamity and permit Ukraine to rebuild. The willingness of Russia to negotiate any deal that fails to meet all its goals however, is a matter of debate.

Russian victory: If Russia eventually emerge in the lead militarily and militarily, it could have the ability to capture portions of Ukraine or install an unofficial government. It would be a major victory for the West as well as Ukraine in general, and will likely lead to a long period of unrest within the region.

Ukrainian victory If Ukraine could finally defeat the Russian invaders, it will be an enormous victory in the fight for democracy and freedom.

The odds are not in your favor however, since Russia has a military that is vastly larger and stronger.

In a long and tense standoff, neither one of the parties could win effectively, and it could last for a long time. The result would be an extremely expensive and devastating ending for everyone involved as well as result in the Ukrainian economy to worsen. The Russian-Ukrainian war's course and appear like in the near future is difficult to forecast without certainty.

The massive assault by Russia against the independent Ukraine is threatening not only Eastern Europe but also the human effort ever since World War II to establish world peace through the law of the land.

To maintain the process of discussion, democracy and diplomacy required to defeat the threat, USIP offers analysis and assistance for actions that could help. The impact of Putin's assault on Ukraine is being all over the world and raises doubts about Russia's potential for aggression in the future. USIP specialists examine whether Russia's activities elsewhere around the world are changing as a result from the war in Ukraine. On February 8, 2023 USIP held a meeting on the reasons why encouraging Ukraine's democratic institutions and processes is crucial for Ukraine can ensure peace for its people and be a vital example of democracy to the rest of the region and further.

On the 8th of November of 2022 USIP held the first Twitter Space discussion about the impact of the immediate and longer-term implications of Russia's shift in position during the Syrian conflict as in the geopolitical consequences of the ongoing conflict within Ukraine in Syria as well as on the Middle East. On the 3rd November 2022 USIP hosted a panel discussion on the latest events in the war and Russia's strategic approach and its consequences on Ukraine, Russia, and Europe along with world-renowned Russia analysts Mark Galeotti. Initiatives to legalize Ukraine in order in order to defend Ukraine's sovereignty as well as give justice to the Ukrainian population was discussed on the 28th of June 2022 by USIP as well as The Ukrainian Embassy. The event was a celebration of Ukrainian Constitution Day, which commemorates the year 1996, which saw the country's ratification of its Constitution. The Right Honorable Pramila Patten, United States Special Representative for Sexual Violence in Conflict.

www.ingramcontent.com/pod-product-compliance
Lightning Source LLC
Chambersburg PA
CBHW070735020526
44118CB00035B/1357